CORE SKILLS

Reading
Comprehension

Martha K. Resnick
Carolyn J. Hyatt
Sylvia E. Freiman

STECK-VAUGHN
ELEMENTARY · SECONDARY · ADULT · LIBRARY

A Harcourt Company

www.svschoolsupply.com

About the Authors

Martha K. Resnick is an experienced elementary teacher, formerly a Reading Resource Teacher with the Baltimore City Schools. She has served as a cooperative practice teacher, training student teachers from many colleges. Mrs. Resnick received her master's degree in education at Loyola College.

Carolyn J. Hyatt has taught elementary, secondary, and adult education classes. She was formerly a Senior Teacher with the Baltimore City Schools. Mrs. Hyatt received her master's degree in education at Loyola College.

Acknowledgments

Designer: Rusty Kaim
Media Researcher: Sarah Fraser
Cover Design: Alexandra Corona
Interior Illustrations: David Cunningham, Sue Durban, Rosemarie Fox-Hicks, and Holly Cooper
Photography: Kenji Kerins, Graphic Masters/ David Roth, PhotoDisc, and Park Street.
Composition: The Clarinda Company

ISBN 0-7398-5730-4
Copyright © 2002 Steck-Vaughn Company

5 6 7 8 9 0 054 06 05 04

Dear Parent,

Welcome to the *Steck-Vaughn Core Skills: Reading Comprehension* series! You have selected a unique book that focuses on developing your child's comprehension skills, the reading and thinking processes associated with the printed word. Because this series was designed by experienced reading professionals, your child will have reading success as well as gain a firm understanding of the necessary skills outlined in national standards.

Reading should be a fun, relaxed activity for children. They should read stories that relate to or build on their own experiences. Vocabulary should be presented in a sequential and logical progression. The stories in this series build on these philosophies to insure your child's reading success. Other important features in this series that will further aid your child include:

- Short reading selections of interest to a young reader.

- Vocabulary introduced in context and repeated often.

- Comprehension skills applied in context to make the reading more relevant.

- Multiple choice exercises that develop skills for standardized test taking.

You may wish to have your child read the selections silently or orally, but you will find that sharing the stories and activities with your child will provide additional confidence and support to succeed. When learners experience success, learning becomes a continuous process moving them onward to higher achievements. Moreover, the more your child reads, the more proficient she or he will become.

Enjoy this special time with your child!

Sincerely,
The Educators and Staff of
Steck-Vaughn School Supply

P.S. You might also like to visit the Special Features section of our website at **www.svschoolsupply.com** for other fun activities and learning suggestions.

Contents

Correlation to Language Arts Content Standards 4

Vocabulary List 5

PART ONE
Story 1 7
A Facts & Inferences
B Vocabulary
C Sequencing
D Using Context Clues

Story 2 11
A Facts & Inferences
B Vocabulary
C Sentence Comprehension
D Vocabulary
E Using Context Clues

Story 3 15
A Facts & Inferences
B Vocabulary
C Sequencing
D Noting Details

Story 4 19
A Facts & Inferences
B Vocabulary
C Using Context Clues
D Drawing Conclusions

Story 5 23
A Facts & Inferences
B Sequencing
C Vocabulary
D Classifying
E Following Directions

Skills Review
(Stories 1–5) 27
A Facts & Inferences
B Vocabulary
C Sequencing
D Drawing Conclusions
E Vocabulary

Story 6 31
A Facts & Inferences
B Vocabulary
C Understanding Conversation
D Picture/Sentence Comprehension

Story 7 35
A Facts & Inferences
B Vocabulary
C Sentence Comprehension

Story 8 39
A Facts & Inferences
B Vocabulary
C Perceiving Relationships
D Using Context Clues

Story 9 43
A Facts & Inferences
B Antonyms
C Drawing Conclusions
D Using Context Clues

Story 10 47
A Facts & Inferences
B Vocabulary
C Main Idea

Skills Review
(Stories 6–10) 51
A Classifying
B Vocabulary
C Perceiving Relationships
D Drawing Conclusions
E Multiple Meanings
F Understanding Conversation
G Main Idea

Story 11 55
A Facts & Inferences
B Noting Details
C Vocabulary
D Main Idea

Story 12 59
A Facts & Inferences
B Vocabulary
C Using a Table of Contents
D Sequencing

Story 13 63
A Facts & Inferences
B Vocabulary
C Using a Picture Dictionary

Story 14 67
A Facts & Inferences
B Vocabulary
C Drawing Conclusions
D Predicting Outcomes

Story 15 71
A Facts & Inferences
B Vocabulary in Context
C Sequencing
D Main Idea

Story 16 75
A Facts & Inferences
B Noting Details
C Picture/Sentence Comprehension

Skills Review
(Stories 11–16) 79
A Drawing Conclusions
B Sequencing
C Using a Picture Dictionary
D Using a Table of Contents
E Drawing Conclusions
F Noting Details

PART TWO

Story 17 84
A Vocabulary
B Facts & Inferences
C Noting Details/Picture Comprehension
D Vocabulary
E Main Idea of Paragraphs
F Noting Details/Sentence Comprehension

Story 18 90
A Facts & Inferences
B Noting Details/Understanding Time Relationships
C Predicting Outcomes
D Vocabulary

Story 19 96
A Facts & Inferences
B Multiple Meanings
C Drawing Conclusions
D Using Context Clues
E Main Idea of Paragraphs
F Sentence Comprehension

Story 20 102
A Facts & Inferences
B Noting Details
C Vocabulary in Context
D Using Context Clues
E Sequencing

Story 21 108
A Facts & Inferences
B & C Understanding Paragraph Structure
D Main Idea
E Picture/Story Comprehension
F Extraneous Sentences in Paragraph
G Vocabulary
H Predicting Outcomes
I Noting Details/Picture Comprehension

Skills Review
(Stories 17–21) 114
A Understanding Paragraph Structure
B Writing a Paragraph
C Picture/Story Comprehension
D Following Directions
E Multiple Meanings
F Using Context Clues
G Vocabulary in Context
H Main Idea of Paragraphs
I Vocabulary

Story 22 120
A Facts & Inferences
B & C Understanding Paragraph Structure
D Vocabulary in Context
E Multiple Meanings
F Writing a Paragraph
G Punctuation
H Drawing Conclusions

Story 23 126
A Facts & Inferences
B Understanding Time Relationships
C Understanding the Calendar
D Sequencing
E Understanding the Calendar
F Vocabulary
G Drawing Conclusions

Story 24 132
A Facts & Inferences
B & C Sequencing
D Vocabulary
E Noting Details
F & G Sequencing

Story 25 138
A Facts & Inferences
B & C Sequencing
D Noting Details/Writing Sentences
E Vocabulary
F Vocabulary in Context
G Sequencing

Story 26 144
A Facts & Inferences
B Vocabulary
C & D Understanding Time Relationships: Seasons
E Understanding Time Relationships: Months
F Following Directions
G Sequencing

Skills Review
(Stories 22–26) 150
A Sequencing
B Vocabulary in Context
C & D Sequencing

Answer Key 154

3

Correlation to Language Arts Content Standards

LANGUAGE ARTS SKILLS	PAGE
Comprehension	
Drawing Conclusions	22, 29, 45, 46, 52, 69, 79, 83, 99, 125, 131
Facts and Inferences	8, 9, 12, 13, 16, 17, 20, 21, 24, 27, 32, 36, 37, 40, 44, 48, 49, 55, 56, 60, 64, 65, 68, 72, 73, 76, 77, 86, 92, 97, 98, 103, 108, 109, 121, 127, 132, 133, 139, 140, 145
Main Idea	50, 54, 58, 74, 88, 100, 101, 110, 119
Noting Details	18, 57, 77, 83, 87, 89, 93, 94, 104, 105, 113, 135, 141
Perceiving Relationships	41, 52
Predicting Outcomes	70, 94, 112
Sentence Comprehension	14, 34, 38, 78, 89, 101, 111, 116
Sequencing	10, 18, 25, 28, 62, 73, 80, 107, 129, 134, 136, 137, 140, 141, 143, 149, 150, 151, 152, 153
Understanding Conversation	33, 53
Vocabulary	
Antonyms	45
Classifying	26, 51
Multiple Meanings	53, 98, 117, 123
Word Meaning	9, 14, 17, 21, 25, 28, 30, 33, 37, 41, 49, 51, 57, 61, 65, 69, 85, 88, 95, 112, 130, 135, 142, 146
Words in Context	10, 13, 14, 22, 42, 46, 73, 100, 106, 118, 119, 123, 142, 143, 150, 151
Research and Study Skills	
Dictionary	66, 81
Following Directions	26, 117, 148
Parts of a Book	61, 82
Understanding Time Relationships/ Calendar Concepts	93, 94, 128, 129, 130, 143, 146, 147, 148, 150, 151
Writing Skills	
Paragraphs	110, 112, 114, 115, 122, 124
Punctuation	124
Sentences	141

Vocabulary

The stories are comprised of words carefully chosen from the Dolch Basic Sight Vocabulary and the Kucera-Francis word list. Words that appear most frequently in primary reading basal series were also used.

   This vocabulary list does not include every word children are expected to read in this book, but rather is a list of words that are introduced as new vocabulary and defined.

Story 1
bills
covered
each
feathers
flippers
heard
laid
met
penguin
several
skinny
stomach
suit
voice
warm

Story 2
another
flash
followed
gills
hungry
parents
right
same
waved

Story 3
eleven
gift
hid
how
kitchen
unhappy

Story 4
beautiful
carrot
drip
floated
melt
mouth
outdoors
sink
sticks

Story 5
across
bumped
line
third
won

Story 6
batter
brother
home run
lap
popcorn
understand

Story 7
became
grew
grow
knew
pumpkin
under
watered

Story 8
before
fallen
here
marks
maybe
tracks
woods

Story 9
after
friend
hurt
nice
nose
pet
someone
try

Story 10
close
eyes
grandmother
hold
those
yard

Story 11
large
mall
morning
picture
pizza
tiny

Story 12
aunt
bathtub
contents
hall
living

Story 13
bite
fool
lily
pad
shook
sticky
stuck
tickle
tongue
zap
zoom

Story 14
buy
candle
counted
enough
sister
week
year

Story 15

afraid
bite
building
city
ears
kites
learns
move
tiger
zip

Story 16

cool
corner
didn't
picnic

Story 17

control
gallop
gentle
hind
jobs
mane
mounted
officer
popular
reins
saddle
stall
wild

Story 18

always
building
frightened
hungry
mashed
quiet
secret
shut
wonderful

Story 19

check
classmate
detective
kind
need
panda
pay
trip
whisper

Story 20

between
cookout
drum
finish
full
grill
hamburger
horn
potato
shape
treasure

Story 21

dollar
felt
hard
July
might
pick
sand
sea
sell
shell

Story 22

air
lucky
octopus
open
playful
spray
swam
through
tiny
whale

Story 23

better
bunkhouse
busy
camp
campfire
floor
month
mop
rain
rode
stung

Story 24

cried
farmer
field
garden
gate
meal
own
teach
wash

Story 25

behind
brake
build
drive
slow
start
tie
twelve
wheel
winter

Story 26

anymore
born
change
different
gloves
jacket
larger
nothing
scarf
strange
summer
warm
wear

6

PART ONE

Look at this animal.
Its feathers look like
a black and white suit.
It walks on two feet.
It has a bill.
It cannot fly, but it swims.
Its flippers help it swim.
It is a penguin, a bird
that lives on ice.

It was a dark, cold winter day. Many penguins left the water and met on the ice. The penguins made a lot of noise. They called to each other.

Mr. Penguin called to Mrs. Penguin. Mrs. Penguin heard his voice. They met and walked.

After several days, Mrs. Penguin laid one egg on the ice. It was time to make a nest for the baby penguin egg.

Mr. Penguin rolled the egg onto his two feet. His stomach feathers covered the egg and kept it warm.

Soon Mrs. Penguin called "Good-by!" She and the other mother penguins went into the sea. They went to eat fish.

The dads stayed on the ice to care for the eggs. They kept the eggs warm for many weeks. They ate nothing. They got very skinny.

One day, the father penguins were talking.

"Where are the mothers?" one penguin asked. "It's time for the eggs to open."

Another penguin said, "I hope they are safe."

Surprise! The next day, the eggs started to open. The little baby penguins began to make noise. The dads were happy.

But where were the mother penguins?

Which one is right? Put a ✔ by it.

1. Where did Mr. Penguin keep his egg?

   _____ a. in the mud

   _____ b. on his feet

   _____ c. on his bill

2. When did the mother penguins go away?

   _____ a. after the babies came out of the eggs

   _____ b. before they laid the eggs

   _____ c. after they laid the eggs

3. While the father penguins held their eggs, when did they eat?

   _____ a. when it was dark

   _____ b. never

   _____ c. when they had an egg sitter

4. Where were the mother penguins?

   _____ a. getting food from the sea

   _____ b. getting skinny

   _____ c. at the store getting food

5. What is a good name for this story?

   _____ a. A Funny Nest

   _____ b. A Nest in a Tree

   _____ c. Mother Penguin Sits on the Eggs

6. When did the penguins meet on the ice?

    ____ a. in the winter

    ____ b. never

    ____ c. when it was warm

7. What is something penguins never do?

    ____ a. swim   ____ b. make noises   ____ c. fly

8. What animals eat penguins?

    ____ a. horses   ____ b. sharks   ____ c. cows

B **Draw lines to match these.**
One is done for you.

1. what your ears did

2. something to put on

3. something very cold

4. very thin

5. what you hear when someone talks

6. what covers all birds

7. more than two

8. where food goes when you eat

ice

stomach

feathers

voice

heard

each

suit

skinny

several

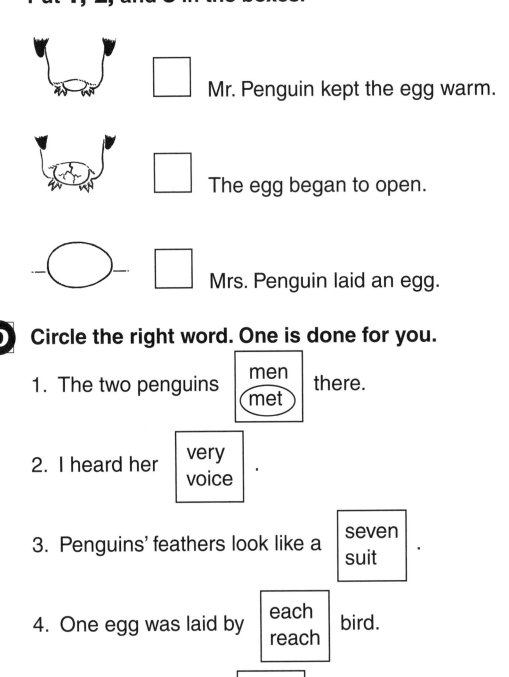

C What happened first? Next? Last?
Put **1, 2,** and **3** in the boxes.

☐ Mr. Penguin kept the egg warm.

☐ The egg began to open.

☐ Mrs. Penguin laid an egg.

D Circle the right word. One is done for you.

1. The two penguins [men / (met)] there.

2. I heard her [very / voice] .

3. Penguins' feathers look like a [seven / suit] .

4. One egg was laid by [each / reach] bird.

5. The eggs must be [worm / warm] .

6. All birds have feathers and [bills / pills] .

2

Surprise! The baby penguins came out of the eggs. Another surprise! The same day, the mother penguins came back from the sea. They were fat from eating many fish. They came back to care for the baby penguins.

Mrs. Penguin saw all the dads and baby penguins. They were all making noise. But Mrs. Penguin knew Mr. Penguin's voice. She walked right to him.

Mr. Penguin said, "Meet our new little girl, Penny."

"Oh," said Mrs. Penguin. "What a pretty little baby she is!"

Baby Penny was hungry. Hungry penguin babies peck on their parents' bills. Then the parents put food in the babies' mouths. Mrs. Penguin fed Baby Penny.

"I'm very hungry, too," said Mr. Penguin. "Now it's my turn to eat."

"We are, too," said all the father penguins. They waved their skinny flippers and said, "Good-by." They all went into the water to find food.

For two weeks, Mr. Penguin and all the father penguins ate fish. They ate fish night and day. They ate fish heads, fish tails, fish fins, and fish gills. They got round and fat. Their stomachs were full.

Then the fathers were ready to swim home. They were ready to help care for the baby penguins.

A shark saw fat Mr. Penguin swimming home. The shark followed Mr. Penguin.

Mr. Penguin moved down, down into the deep water. The shark went swimming after him.

Quick as a flash, Mr. Penguin zoomed up, up. His flippers moved as fast as the wind.

He rolled onto his stomach. He slid through the water right up to the icy shore.

The hungry shark's mouth opened. He reached for Mr. Penguin's tail feathers. The shark was unlucky. Mr. Penguin, quick as a flash, slid out of the water. He zoomed over the ice on his stomach.

He heard Mrs. Penguin's voice. He heard Baby Penny's voice. He slid right over to them.

A **Which one is right? Put a ✔ by it.**

1. How was Mrs. Penguin different when she came back?

   _____ a. She was round and fat.

   _____ b. She was very skinny.

   _____ c. She was hungry.

2. When did Mr. Penguin go to eat?

   _____ a. the week before the egg opened

   _____ b. when the egg was on his feet

   _____ c. after the egg opened

3. Why did Mr. Penguin go away from Mrs. Penguin?

_____ a. He wanted to play.

_____ b. He needed a new suit.

_____ c. He needed food.

4. Why do you think Mr. Penguin slid on his stomach?

_____ a. His feet hurt.

_____ b. It was quicker than walking on ice.

_____ c. It was the only way he could move.

5. What is the best name for this story?

_____ a. Penny Gets Away from a Shark

_____ b. The Baby Penguin Turns Around

_____ c. Mr. and Mrs. Penguin Take Turns

B **Read the words in the Word Box. Read the sentences. Write the word that belongs in each sentence.**

Word Box	flippers followed	parents another	waved

1. The baby _____ his parents.

2. Penguins swim with their _____ .

3. The moms _____ good-by.

4. Your mom and dad are your _____ .

13

C **Read the sentences. Put an X next to ones that are not right. Put a ✔ next to the ones that are right.**

_____ 1. Penguins have warm fur.

_____ 2. Mother penguins keep the eggs on their feet.

_____ 3. The parents take turns helping the baby.

_____ 4. Penguins fly quickly.

_____ 5. Penguins' feathers are black and white.

_____ 6. The penguin slid on his stomach quick as a flash.

D **Here is a penguin. Draw a line from each word to its picture.**

1. bill

2. head

3. stomach

4. flipper

5. feet

6. tail

E **Circle the right word.**

1. The penguins waved their | flippers / followed | .

2. Mrs. Penguin did not come back the | some / same | day.

3. Penguins swim quick as a | feather / flash | .

4. Fish have | gills / bills | .

14

Sunday afternoon Pedro said, "I will not go! I do not want to go to Nita's party!"

"Why not?" asked his mother.

Pedro told her, "Nita asked **nine** girls and **two** boys to come."

Mother said, "Think how unhappy the other boy will be if you are not there."

"I don't care!" yelled Pedro.

But his mother took him to the door. She gave him the gift for Nita.

"Good-bye, Pedro," Mother said.

Then Pedro went around to the kitchen door. No one saw him go back into the house.

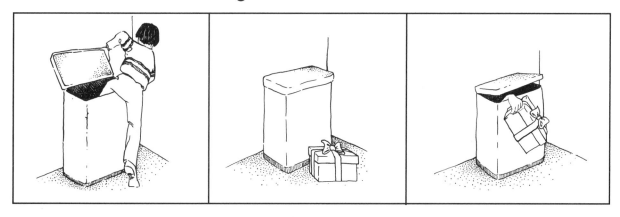

Chico, the dog, walked by.

Mother hugged Chico. Father hugged Chico. They said, "What a good dog."

Pedro said, "I can never hide from Chico!"

15

1. What did Pedro do first?

_____ a. He hid.

_____ b. He said, "I do not want to go."

_____ c. He went in the back door.

2. Where did Chico go?

_____ a. to Nita's party

_____ b. to the doghouse

_____ c. to a woman and a man

3. Why didn't Pedro want to go?

_____ a. too many gifts

_____ b. too many boys

_____ c. too many girls

4. Why did Pedro get a gift for Nita?

_____ a. It was Nita's birthday.

_____ b. Nita was very sick.

_____ c. Nita was going away.

5. When was the party?

_____ a. morning

_____ b. afternoon

_____ c. night

6. What day was the party?

_____ a. Saturday   _____ b. Sunday   _____ c. Friday

7. How did Chico know where Pedro was?

_____ a. Mother told him.

_____ b. Pedro told him.

_____ c. He smelled Pedro.

8. What is the best name for this story?

_____ a. Pedro Hides

_____ b. Looking for Chico

_____ c. Nita's Gift

B **Draw lines to match these. One is done for you.**

1. go where no one can see you

2. not this one

3. said a question

4. comes after ten

5. not in front

asked

how

hide

eleven

other

back

What happened first? Next? Last? Put 1, 2, 3, 4, and 5 in the boxes.

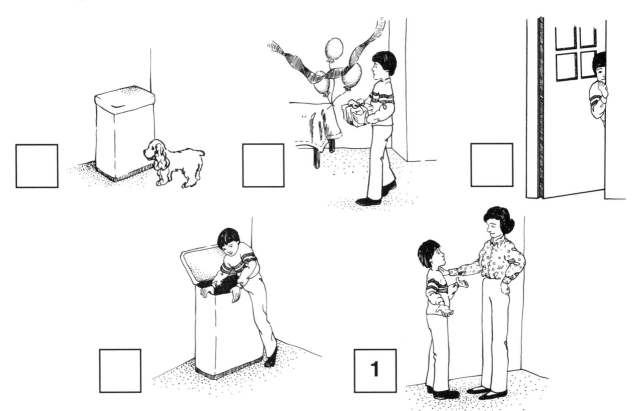

Write yes or no.

1. Nita is the pet dog. _____
2. Pedro has two feet. _____
3. Chico can read a book. _____
4. The gift was for Nita. _____
5. Nita asked nine girls to the party. _____
6. Mother took Chico to the party. _____
7. Chico found Pedro. _____

Tuesday Sally and Sam were playing outdoors in the snow. They made a little snowman.

The snowman's eyes were buttons. His nose was a carrot. His mouth was two sticks.

"Let's put a cap on his head," said Sally. "He is beautiful!"

"The sun is out," said Sam. "It can melt the snowman."

The children took the little snowman into the kitchen. They stopped up the sink. They put him in the sink. They put ice all around him.

"He will not melt now," laughed Sam.

"Let's go play at Yong Cha's house until Dad comes home," said Sally. Out they ran.

All afternoon Sally and Sam were gone. Drip, drip went the water into the sink. Melt, melt went the snowman in the sink.

When Dad and the children came home, they saw a sink full of water. A carrot and two buttons floated in the water.

What do you think happened? What do you think they had to do?

A **Which one is right? Put a ✓ by it.**

1. What did the children do first?

_____ a. They went to Yong Cha's house.

_____ b. They took a snowman into the kitchen.

_____ c. They put a cap on the snowman.

2. Why was the snowman in the kitchen?

_____ a. to keep the kitchen cold

_____ b. to keep the snowman from melting

_____ c. to keep the snowman warm

3. What was a nose for the snowman?

_____ a. a button

_____ b. a carrot

_____ c. a stick

4. Where did the children go?

_____ a. to get Dad

_____ b. to school

_____ c. to play with a friend

5. What was floating in the sink?

_____ a. a carrot and two buttons

_____ b. a button and a boot

_____ c. a carrot and a boot

6. Which picture do you think fits the end of the story?

_____ a.   b.   _____ c.

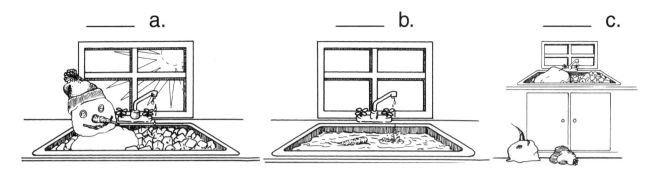

7. What do you think Sally and Sam had to do next?

_____ a. go swimming

_____ b. take a bath

_____ c. clean the sink

8. What is the story about?

_____ a. making a snowman with Dad

_____ b. a talking snowman

_____ c. the sun melting a snowman

B **Draw lines to match these.**

1. good to look at   sink

2. becomes water   beautiful

3. an orange food   outdoors

4. a part of you   float

5. stay on top of the water   melts

6. not in the house   drip

7. It holds water in the kitchen.   carrot

nose   **21**

Circle the right word. One is done for you.

1. Dad said, " go with you."

2. Sally said, " my snowman."

3. Sam said, " go to Yong Cha's house."

4. Dad said, "Come home with ."

5. They said, " must stop the water."

D **Read about where each child lives. Then write the first letter of the child's name on the right house.**

Sam and Sally live on Blue Street. Their friends live on Blue Street, too.

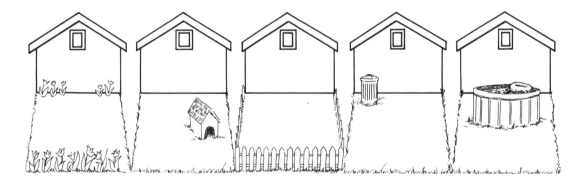

1. Carlos said, "My house has a fence around it."

2. Kim said, "You can swim in back of my house."

3. Sam said, "We have a doghouse out back."

4. Yong Cha said, "I live next door to Sam."

5

Last Saturday there was a boat race. Eight boats were in it. The boats had to race across the lake. Boats that got to the other side first were winners.

The boats were in a line. They started off in a hurry. A big red boat went fast. A yellow boat went faster. The other boats were in back of them.

Then a fire started on the red boat. People stopped the red boat to put out the fire.

The white boat went too near the land. It got in the mud. It did not get across the lake.

The yellow boat bumped into the brown boat. They were out of the race.

A pink boat got to the other side first. The green boat came in second. Next came a purple boat. It was third. An old orange boat was the last in the race.

All the boats that got across the lake were winners. People on those boats won some money.

1. What is this story about?

_____ a. children in a race

_____ b. a boat race

_____ c. a car race

2. Where was this race?

_____ a. on a playground

_____ b. on a street

_____ c. in the water

3. How many boats had to stop?

_____ a. four _____ b. three _____ c. eight

4. What happened to the white boat?

_____ a. It had a fire.

_____ b. It came in first.

_____ c. It got in the mud.

5. What happened to the brown boat?

_____ a. It went too near the land.

_____ b. It was hit by the yellow boat.

_____ c. It had a fire.

6. What did the winners get?

_____ a. cups _____ b. money _____ c. boats

B How did they come in? Color the boats.
Write the names of the colors.

1. first	2. second	3. third	4. last
_____	_____	_____	_____

 C Draw lines to match these.

1. some water   bumped

2. ran into something   third

3. something very hot   across

4. a color   lake

5. after the first two   Saturday

6. the one that comes in first   orange

7. from one side to the other   fire

8. a row of things   winner

                                       line

D Put an **X** on the word that does not belong.
One is done for you.

1. Wednesday	Monday	~~spring~~	Saturday
2. runner	winner	player	butter
3. lake	pond	boat	water
4. third	tiger	dog	worm
5. ten	three	tree	nine
6. grass	tree	second	flower
7. boat	fire	car	bus

E Fun Time! Can you do this?

1. Color the second boat pink.
2. Put a ✔ on the next to the last one.
3. Color the first boat purple.
4. Put an **X** under the last boat.
5. Color the third boat orange.
6. Put a box around the second boat.
7. Color the tall boats in the middle green.
8. How many boats did you color green? _____

SKILLS REVIEW (Stories 1–5)

 A **Read this story. Check the right answers.**

One warm day, Carlos and Pedro were at the zoo.
A zoo helper was showing the people a father penguin.
The dad had no egg to take care of. The zoo helper
put a hot dog roll next to the father penguin. The father
penguin put it on his feet. His feathers kept it warm.

The zoo helper said, "The penguin wants a baby to
come out of the roll."

Pedro, Carlos, and all the people laughed.

1. What do you think happened next?

_____ a. A baby penguin came out of the roll.

_____ b. The penguin made a nest for the roll.

_____ c. A baby seal came out of the roll.

2. What do you know about Carlos and Pedro?

_____ a. They lived in a zoo.

_____ b. They ate hot dogs at the zoo.

_____ c. They had fun at the zoo.

3. When did this story happen?

_____ a. one cold night

_____ b. one warm night

_____ c. one warm day

B **Here is a snowman. Draw a line from each word to its picture.**

1. buttons

2. head

3. carrot

4. eyes

5. sticks

6. nose

7. cap

8. mouth

C **Write the names of the children next to the pictures.**

1. _____

2. _____

3. _____

4. _____

5. _____

6. _____

1. Jill is next to the last.

2. Sam is right after the third.

3. Pedro is the first.

4. Sally is the second.

5. Dan is the last.

6. Andy is not here.

7. Ann is the third.

D **Can you guess the riddles? Circle the right words.**

1. It is wet. It can be hot or cold.
   You can drink it. It is in food.
   You can give it to flowers.
   What is it?

   milk   water   dog

2. It is on you. It helps you eat. It
   helps you talk. What is it?

   milk   melt   mouth

3. I have four feet and a tail.
   Sometimes I take care of the house.
   I can be black or white or brown.
   I wag my tail and say, "Bow-bow."
   I like to play with a ball.
   What am I?

   a dog   a bird   an ant

4. Sometimes I have it. Sometimes you
   have it. I can give it to someone.
   Someone can give it to you. No one
   likes to get it. It makes you sick.
   What is it?

   a hot dog   a cold   a hot

E **Read the words in the Word Box.**
Write the words next to the meanings.

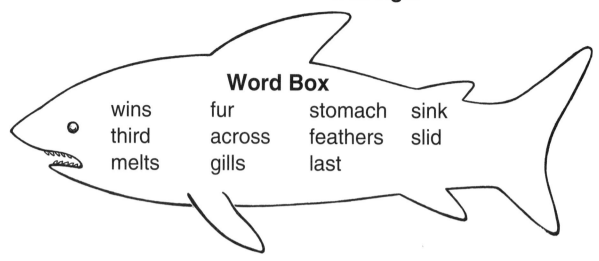

Word Box

wins	fur	stomach	sink
third	across	feathers	slid
melts	gills	last	

1. comes after second   _____

2. from side to side   _____

3. a part of your body   _____

4. a part of a fish   _____

5. something in the kitchen   _____

6. becomes water   _____

7. comes in first   _____

8. what covers a bird   _____

9. what covers cats   _____

10. at the end of the line   _____

On Thursday evening, Janet took her little brother, Jay, to the big ball park. Jay was eight years old. Jay didn't understand the ball game. But he liked to sit outdoors and yell. He liked to eat hot dogs and popcorn.

Jay had a hot dog in one hand. He had a box of popcorn in his lap. He had a hot dog next to him, too. Jay was very happy.

The batter hit the ball. The ball came flying over to the people.

"It's a home run!" yelled all the people.

"I want to get that ball!" yelled Janet.

People got ready to grab the ball. Everyone wanted to catch the ball. But not Jay! He was eating. He did not want to catch the ball.

Down came the ball! Did it fly into the hands waiting for it? No! It came down on Jay's lap on top of his popcorn! The hot dog and popcorn fell to the ground. But Jay had the ball!

"The boy who didn't want the ball got it!" said Janet.

All Jay said was, "Let's get more popcorn!"

Ⓐ Which one is right? Put a ✔ by it.

1. When did they go to the ball game?

_____ a. morning _____ b. noon _____ c. night

2. How old was Jay?

_____ a. seven _____ b. nine _____ c. eight

3. Why did Jay go to the ball game?

_____ a. to eat hot dogs and popcorn

_____ b. to get a ball

_____ c. to play ball

4. Where did the ball go?

_____ a. out of the ball park

_____ b. into Janet's hands

_____ c. into Jay's lap

5. What do you think happened next?

_____ a. Jay started to cry.

_____ b. Jay let Janet have the ball.

_____ c. Jay hit a home run.

6. What is the best name for this story?

_____ a. The Ball Hits Janet

_____ b. A Surprise Hot Dog

_____ c. A Surprise Ball

B **Draw lines to match these.**

1. to know all about

2. a white food

3. what your legs make
   when you sit down

4. one who hits the
   ball with a bat

5. a ball hit very far

6. a boy in your family

7. not in the house

understand

brother

popcorn

home run

lap

outdoors

grab

batter

C **Who is talking? Write the name.**

_____ 1. "That is not a home run," said Jay
to Janet.

_____ 2. "Jay, we will go this evening,"
said Janet.

_____ 3. Jay said, "I don't understand this
game, Janet."

_____ 4. "Catch that ball!" yelled Janet. "Jay,
help catch it!"

_____ 5. "No, Janet," said Jay, "that is not my
hot dog."

D Find the sentence that goes with each picture.
Write the letter on the line.

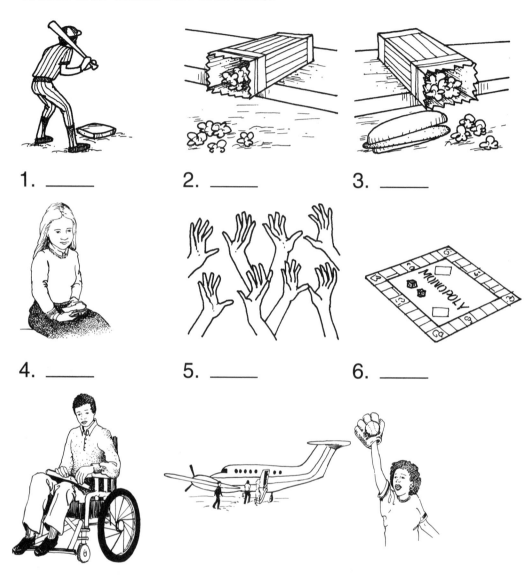

1. _____

2. _____

3. _____

4. _____

5. _____

6. _____

7. _____

8. _____

9. _____

a. This game does not use a ball.
b. The food is on her lap.
c. The batter is ready to hit the ball.
d. The book is on his lap.
e. Everyone wants to catch the ball.
f. The people are getting ready to swim.
g. The popcorn and hot dog fell to the ground.
h. Someone is catching the ball.
i. The people are getting ready to fly.
j. The popcorn fell to the ground.

34

One spring day, Ann and Andy were planting seeds. Their little brother, Billy, did not want to help.

A woman came by. She looked at Billy and said, "Here are five seeds. If you plant the five seeds, you will get a big surprise."

Billy wanted to know what the surprise was. He planted the seeds in back of the dog house.

Soon three little plants came up. Little leaves were on them. Billy watered them every day. The plants got bigger. They got big leaves on them. Then they began to go all over the ground like this.

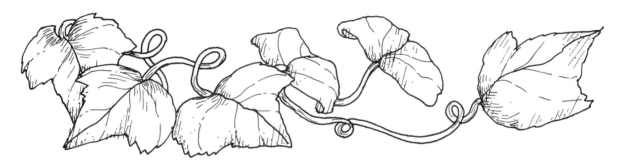

Then pretty yellow flowers came out on the plants. Under the flowers were little green balls. Every day the green balls got bigger. Then the green balls became yellow.

Soon the yellow balls were very, very big. Now they became orange. They looked like this.

Billy and the children laughed. They saw what the big surprise was.

Do you know what Billy had planted?

A **Which one is right? Put a ✔ by it.**

1. What were the surprise plants?

   _____ a. water plants

   _____ b. pumpkins

   _____ c. new flowers

2. How many of Billy's seeds did not grow?

   _____ a. five   _____ b. three   _____ c. two

3. Why did Billy plant the seeds?

   _____ a. He liked to see flowers come up.

   _____ b. He wanted to know what the surprise was.

   _____ c. He wanted to help his family.

4. Where did Billy get the seeds?

   _____ a. at the store

   _____ b. from his mother

   _____ c. from a woman

5. What came out of the plants first?

   _____ a. leaves

   _____ b. flowers

   _____ c. yellow balls

6. What color were the flowers?

   _____ a. white   _____ b. yellow   _____ c. pink

7. Where did Billy plant the seeds?

     _____ a. in a window box

     _____ b. under a tree

     _____ c. in back of the dog house

8. What is the best name for this story?

     _____ a. The Pretty Yellow Flowers

     _____ b. The Pretty Woman

     _____ c. The Surprise Plants

B **Draw lines to match these.**

1. said, "Ha, ha, ha!"

2. an orange food

3. a girl who grew up

4. nice to look at

5. thing a plant grows from

6. grew into

7. land we walk on

8. putting it into the ground to grow

woman

brother

laughed

pumpkin

planting

pretty

ground

seed

became

C **Find the sentence that means the same as the first one. Put a ✔ by it.**

1. Billy, Ann, and Andy were planting seeds.

   _____ a. They were putting seeds in the ground.

   _____ b. She was putting seeds in the ground.

2. Five little seeds were in the woman's hand.

   _____ a. The woman had a seed in her hand.

   _____ b. The woman had some seeds in her hand.

3. Billy watered the plants every day.

   _____ a. Billy put water on the plants two times.

   _____ b. Billy put water on the plants day after day.

4. The seeds were planted in the spring.

   _____ a. The seeds were planted in the summer.

   _____ b. The seeds were planted before summer.

5. The yellow flowers fell off. Under them were little green balls.

   _____ a. Little green balls were under the flowers.

   _____ b. The green balls became yellow flowers.

6. The children found out what the surprise was.

   _____ a. The children knew that the surprise seeds were pumpkin seeds.

   _____ b. The children did not know what the seeds were.

On Thursday snow fell. Marcy and Dan went outdoors. The trees and grass were white with snow. The children's boots made marks in the snow. Dan looked back to see them.

"Our boots make funny tracks in the snow," said Dan.

"Look over there," said Marcy. "An animal has walked here before us."

They saw tracks in the snow.

"Let's see where the animal went," said Dan.

"Maybe we can find out what animal makes tracks like these," said Marcy.

The children followed the tracks into the woods. The tracks went over to an old tree that had fallen to the ground.

"Look under that tree!" said Dan. "It's a pretty little black and white cat."

"Let's take the cat home. It must be very cold," said Marcy.

The children ran to the old tree. But they stopped before they got up to it.

"Oh! Oh!" they yelled. "That's no cat! Let's get away from here."

Dan said, "If we get too near to it, we may smell a very bad smell."

What animal had made the tracks in the snow?

A. Which one is right? Put a ✔ by it.

1. What animal did they see?

_____ a. cat _____ b. squirrel _____ c. skunk

2. How did they know an animal was near by?

_____ a. They saw its tracks.

_____ b. They could hear it walking.

_____ c. The animal said, "Mew, mew."

3. Where did they see the animal?

_____ a. in the leaves

_____ b. under an old tree

_____ c. under a fence

4. When did the snow fall?

_____ a. Monday _____ b. Thursday _____ c. Friday

5. What can this animal do if you get too near?

_____ a. It can bark at you.

_____ b. It can bite you.

_____ c. It can let out a bad smell.

6. What is the best name for this story?

_____ a. An Animal's Spots

_____ b. The Tracks of the Skunk

_____ c. The Tracks of the Fox

Draw lines to match these.

fallen

followed

1. the day before Friday

funny

2. marks that feet make

smell

3. down on the ground

skunk

4. went in back of

Thursday

5. place with many trees

tracks

6. animal with four feet

woods

7. making us laugh

C **What do you know about skunks?**
Circle the right ones.

1. Which is the skunk?

2. How many feet do skunks have?	two	four
3. Do skunks talk?	yes	no
4. Do skunks read?	yes	no
5. Do skunks have green spots?	yes	no
6. Can we ride on a skunk?	yes	no
7. Are skunks white and black?	yes	no
8. Do skunks put on boots?	yes	no

D Circle the right word for each story.

1. The skunk did not want people to catch her.
   She went under the fallen tree.
   She _____ there.

         had   hid   did

2. The big bear ran to the old tree. A skunk lived
   in the old tree. The bear surprised her. Then
   the skunk surprised the bear! She let out a
   bad _____.

         sell   spell   smell

3. There was an old tree by Dan's window. Every
   morning Dan looked at it. One day the tree
   was not there. It was on the ground. The tree
   had _____ down.

         fallen   rested   smelled

4. White snow was all over the ground. Dan put on
   his hat and coat. He went out to play. He could
   not walk in the snow. Dan said, "I forgot
   my _____."

         books   boots   bugs

5. Marcy walked in the snow. Her boots made marks
   where she walked. Dan wanted to find Marcy.
   Dan found her by looking at Marcy's _____.

         trees   backs   tracks

Why don't people like us?
We are pretty animals. We
help people.

We help by eating bugs
that hurt people. We eat
rats and mice, too. We
hunt for food at night. We
eat things that people do
not want.

We never try to get into
houses as mice do. We
never run after people as
tigers do. We do not climb
trees as squirrels do.

We skunks like to be
with other skunks. We do
not try to live with people.
We stay away from other
animals. We live in old
trees or under the ground.

We smell good if you do
not put your hands on us.
Be careful near us, and
you will not smell us. We
let out our bad smell if
someone wants to hurt us.

We want you to be
careful and not run after
us. Stay away from us, and
we will stay away from you.
But we like to help you.
Please like us!

A Which one is right? Put a ✔ by it.

1. When do skunks come out to eat?

_____ a. morning _____ b. noon _____ c. night

2. What would a skunk eat?

_____ a. a fly _____ b. a bag _____ c. a house

3. How do skunks help people?

_____ a. by looking pretty

_____ b. by eating mice

_____ c. by smelling nice

4. When will a skunk smell bad?

_____ a. when you try to catch it

_____ b. all the time

_____ c. never

5. What do skunks want people to do for them?

_____ a. play with them

_____ b. keep away from them

_____ c. bring them into the house

6. What is the best name for this story?

_____ a. A Bad Animal

_____ b. A Careful Animal

_____ c. Helpers to People

B **Draw lines to match the opposites.**
One is done for you.

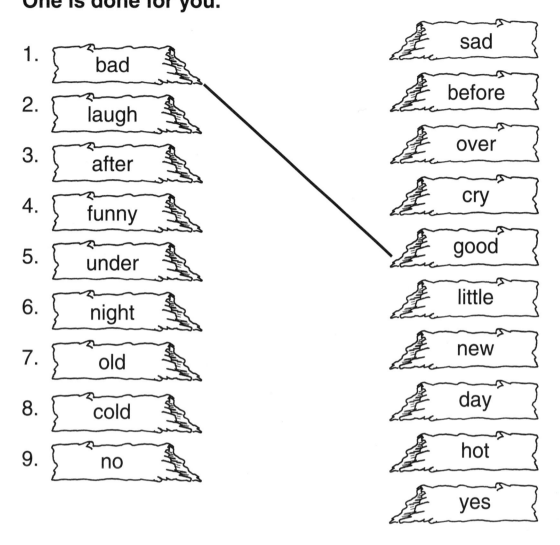

1. bad
2. laugh
3. after
4. funny
5. under
6. night
7. old
8. cold
9. no

sad
before
over
cry
good
little
new
day
hot
yes

C **Can you guess the riddles? Circle the right word.**

1. This is an animal.
   It has four feet.
   It is a friend to us.
   You may have one
   as a pet.
   It eats mice.
   It says, "Mew, mew."
   What is it?

   cow   skunk   cat

2. This is a place.
   Many trees are here.
   Many animals live here.
   Skunks and birds are
   here.
   Bugs, worms, and ants
   live here, too.
   What is this place?

   store   woods   school

3. This is someone who likes you.
   It is someone that you like, too.
   This someone helps you.
   It is someone you want to help.
   This someone will not hurt you.
   Who is it?

   friend   fire   four

4. This is on you. It smells things.
   It can smell food cooking.
   It can smell pretty flowers.
   It can get red and cold in winter.
   What is it?

   mouth   ear   nose

D **Which is the right word? Circle it.**

1. Some animals can _____ fast.

   swim   swimming

2. Skunks help us by _____ bugs that hurt us.

   eat   eating

3. A skunk likes to _____ with other skunks.

   stay   staying

4. The skunk let out a bad _____ at the fox.

   smell   smelling

5. Skunks _____ for food at night.

   hunt   hunting

6. Some people _____ skunks are pretty.

   think   thinking

Tom, Bob, and Jack were going fishing on Friday afternoon. They went out that morning to dig up some worms. The boys put the worms into a can. They left the can on the kitchen table. Jack's grandmother saw the worms.

"Oh, no!" yelled Grandmother. "Get those things out of here!"

Jack said, "Don't you like worms, Grandmother?"

"No!" said Grandmother. The boys laughed.

After lunch, the three boys left to go fishing. They saw Betty and Jill.

"Let's see if the girls will yell," said Bob.

"Let's put worms on them," said Tom. "It will be so funny."

Jack said to the girls, "Close your eyes. Hold out your hands. I have something for you."

Jill and Betty put out their hands. Jack pulled four worms out of the can. He put two worms in each girl's hands.

Then the boys got a surprise. Betty and Jill did not run or yell! They held the worms.

"Don't you want us to take away the worms?" asked Jack. "Grandmother didn't like them."

"No, we like worms," said the girls.

Betty and Jill took the four worms and went fishing.

A **Which one is right? Put a ✔ by it.**

1. When did this happen?

_____ a. Sunday   _____ b. Friday   _____ c. Tuesday

2. When did the boys dig up the worms?

_____ a. morning   _____ b. afternoon   _____ c. night

3. What is the story about?

_____ a. The boys got a lot of fish.

_____ b. Grandmother surprised the girls.

_____ c. The girls surprised the boys.

4. Where did Grandmother see the worms?

_____ a. in the yard

_____ b. in the girls' hands

_____ c. on the table

5. Why did Grandmother yell?

_____ a. The worms got away.

_____ b. She did not like worms.

_____ c. The boys were eating worms.

6. When did the boys eat lunch?

_____ a. before they got the worms

_____ b. after they went fishing

_____ c. after they got the worms

7. What did the girls do with the worms?

_____ a. yelled at them

_____ b. put them back in the can

_____ c. went fishing

8. What does this story show us?

_____ a. Everyone likes worms.

_____ b. No one likes worms.

_____ c. Some people like worms.

9. What is the best name for this story?

_____ a. How Worms Help Us

_____ b. How To Fish

_____ c. Who Likes Worms?

B **Draw lines to match these.**

1. a little animal

2. your mother's mother

3. comes after Thursday

4. keep something in your hand

5. to shut

6. went away

fishing

Friday

grandmother

left

worm

close

hold

C **What is going on in the picture? Put an X by the sentence that goes with the picture.**

1.
_____ a. Four cans are on the table.

_____ b. Three cans are in the yard.

_____ c. Two cans are on the table.

2.
_____ a. A girl is pulling a worm.

_____ b. A grandmother is pulling flowers.

_____ c. A bird is pulling a worm.

3.
_____ a. The boys held some fish.

_____ b. The boys held some worms.

_____ c. The fish held some boys.

4.
_____ a. Flowers are in the back yard.

_____ b. Fish are in the back yard.

_____ c. Grandmother is in the back yard.

5.
_____ a. Fish are swimming in the water.

_____ b. Fish are yelling in the water.

_____ c. Worms are swimming in the water.

A Why are these words together? Pick a name for these words from the box. Write the names on the right lines.

numbers	foods	people
places	colors	animals

1. _____

brother   woman
batter   children
grandmother

2. _____

popcorn   fish
oranges   pumpkin
hotdog

3. _____

ball park   woods
kitchen   school

4. _____

black   white
orange   yellow

B Draw lines to match these.

1. boy in your family

2. said, "Ha, ha!"

3. not in the house

4. girl who grew up

5. day before Friday

6. to shut

outdoors

orange

close

brother

woman

laughed

Thursday

C **What do you know about skunks and worms?**
Circle the right ones.

1. Which one will let out a bad smell?

  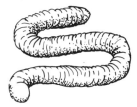 

2. Do skunks have two tails?   yes   no

3. Does a skunk fly at night?   yes   no

4. Are skunks land animals?   yes   no

5. Can skunks help people?   yes   no

6. Can a worm eat a fish?   yes   no

7. Do worms run very fast?   yes   no

8. Do worms hide in the grass?   yes   no

9. Can we ride on a worm?   yes   no

D **Can you guess the riddles? Circle the right word.**

1. This is very hot.
   It looks yellow.
   It helps plants grow.
   We see it in the day.
   What is it?

   sun   moon   snow

2. It is cold and white.
   Put it in a cup.
   It is good to drink.
   We get it from cows.
   What is it?

   snow   rain   milk

3. This animal is careful.
   It never runs too fast.
   It pulls its legs and
   head into its shell.
   What is it?

   skunk   turtle   squirrel

4. This animal likes trees.
   It climbs to tree tops.
   It eats nuts.
   It lives in the park.
   What is it?

   turtle   squirrel   skunk

E **Circle the one word that fits both sentences.**

cold   hold   sold

1. Get a good _____ on the rope.

2. Can you _____ any more food?

_____

plant   place   play

3. Put some water on the lettuce _____.

4. Let's _____ some pumpkin seeds.

_____

far   fell   fall

5. This _____ we will rake the leaves.

6. Did you _____ down on the playground?

F **Who is talking? Write the name.**

_____ 1. "Don't you like worms,
Grandmother?" asked Jack.

_____ 2. Betty said to Jill, "I see Tom,
Bob, and Jack over there."

_____ 3. Bob said, "Let's see if Betty
and Jill will yell."

_____ 4. "Do you want us to take away the
worms, Betty?" asked Tom.

_____ 5. "No," said Jill, "Betty and I like
worms."

G **What is funny about the pictures? Put a ✔ by the funny sentences.**

1. _____ a. The mice are going across the lake on a pumpkin.

   _____ b. The mice are going across the lake on a boat.

2. _____ a. The skunk left its tracks in the snow.

   _____ b. The skunk's tracks look like hands.

3. _____ a. The worm is eating the fish.

   _____ b. The fish is eating the worm.

4. _____ a. Father Robin gives the bird a worm.

   _____ b. Father Robin gives the tiger a worm.

5. _____ a. Jay has a bat in his hot dog bun.

   _____ b. Jay has a hot dog to eat.

54

Karen, Mai, and Ann went to the mall on Saturday morning. They wanted to get some T-shirts. Karen's big brother Ray took the girls in his new car. They got there at eleven o'clock.

"I'll be back to pick you up at two o'clock," said Ray. "Meet me here at the Water Street door."

The three friends walked around the mall. They looked in some stores. They had some pizza at the food stand. Then they went to the T-shirt store.

Karen liked to swim. She saw a T-shirt with a picture of a large penguin. "That's for me!" she said.

Mai's shirt had a picture of a tiny fox. Ann got one with a shark.

It was almost two o'clock. The girls ran fast to the Water Street door. They were just in time. Ray was just getting there.

A **Which one is right? Put a ✓ by it.**

1. Why did the girls go to the mall?

_____ a. They went to help Karen's brother.

_____ b. They wanted to get new T-shirts.

_____ c. It was a rainy day.

2. What time do you think the girls went to the mall?

_____ a. at night

_____ b. on Sunday

_____ c. in the morning

3. What is the best title for this story?

_____ a. Fun at the Mall

_____ b. Ray's New Shoes

_____ c. A Rainy Walk Home

4. What happened first in the story?

_____ a. The girls got their names on T-shirts.

_____ b. The girls ate.

_____ c. The girls ran to the Water Street door.

5. When did the girls have to meet Ray?

_____ a. at five o'clock

_____ b. at two o'clock

_____ c. at eleven o'clock

6. What meal did the girls eat at the mall?

_____ a. ice cream _____ b. lunch _____ c. dinner

7. How did the girls go into the mall?

_____ a. at the big blue door

_____ b. at the door on Beach Street

_____ c. at the door on Water Street

B Write each girl's name on her T-shirt. Detective Sharp-Eye says, "Look back in the story. Find the clues. Which T-shirt do you think belongs to Ann? Which to Karen? Which to Mai?"

1. 2. 3.

C Draw lines to match these.

1. a place with many stores

2. something to eat

3. the opposite of small

4. something you draw

5. very, very small

6. one more than ten

7. comes before the afternoon

8. a place to go in and out

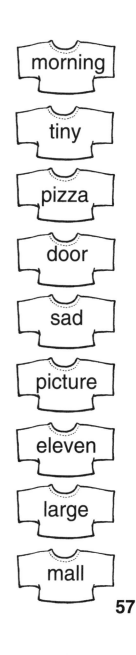

morning

tiny

pizza

door

sad

picture

eleven

large

mall

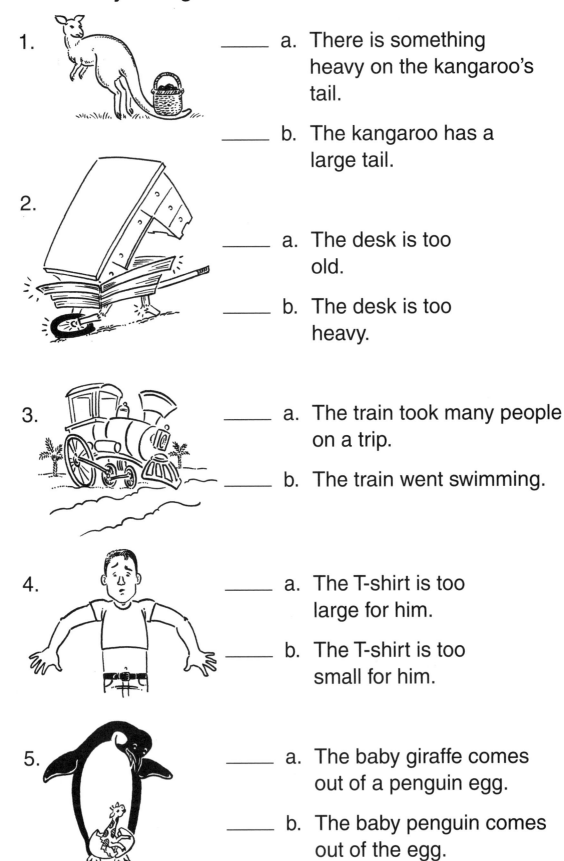

D **What is funny about the pictures?**
Put a ✔ by the right sentences.

1.
_____ a. There is something heavy on the kangaroo's tail.

_____ b. The kangaroo has a large tail.

2.
_____ a. The desk is too old.

_____ b. The desk is too heavy.

3.
_____ a. The train took many people on a trip.

_____ b. The train went swimming.

4.
_____ a. The T-shirt is too large for him.

_____ b. The T-shirt is too small for him.

5.
_____ a. The baby giraffe comes out of a penguin egg.

_____ b. The baby penguin comes out of the egg.

On Tuesday evening, the family got home at eight o'clock. There was something on the door.

I was here, but you were out. I hid a surprise gift for you. Look for it.
Love,
Aunt May

The family looked everywhere. Randy hunted in the kitchen. Peggy and Mom ran to the bedroom. Dad hunted in the living room. They all went into the hall. They found nothing!

Then everyone heard something. It came from the bathtub. When the family ran in, they saw

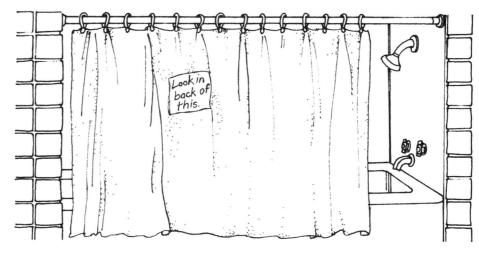

Look in back of this.

This was their surprise gift!

A **Which one is right? Put a ✔ by it.**

1. What were Randy and Peggy looking for?

_____ a. Aunt May   _____ b. a surprise

2. Which sentence is right?

_____ a. Aunt May did not leave a surprise.

_____ b. Aunt May did not get in the house.

_____ c. Aunt May got into the house.

3. Where did the family forget to look?

_____ a. in the living room

_____ b. in the tub

_____ c. on the kitchen sink

4. What happened first?

_____ a. Aunt May got to the house.

_____ b. The family came home.

_____ c. They found an animal.

5. Who looked in the living room?

_____ a. Dad   _____ b. May   _____ c. Peggy

6. What is the best name for this story?

_____ a. A Ball in the Kitchen

_____ b. A New Living Room

_____ c. A Bird in the Bathtub

B **Draw lines to match these.**

aunt

1. a place for a bath   tub

2. put where no one could see   hall

3. something the ears did   heard

4. part of a house   yard

5. Mom's sister   hid

6. something around the house   gift

C **Here is the Table of Contents page of a book. Use it to answer the questions.**

1. On which page will you

   find *Mr. Robin*? _____

2. On which page is the
   last story in the book? _____

3. How many stories are in

   this book? _____

4. On which page does

   A Surprise start? _____

5. Which story starts on page 2?

Stories

The New Birdbath. . . 2

A Surprise 4

Mr. Robin 7

The Fence Fell 10

D Peggy and Randy looked for something. They went all around the house. Look at this map to see how they went. Follow the numbers. Circle the words below that tell where they went.

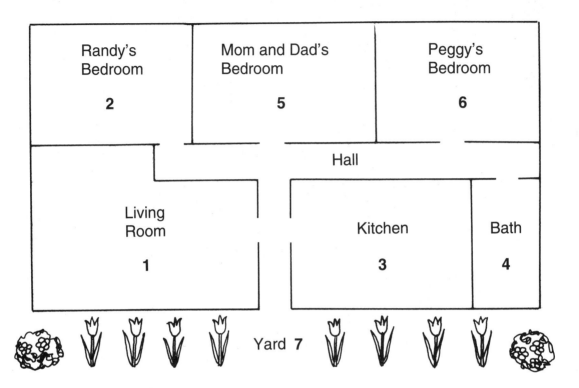

1. Where did they go first?

    living room   kitchen   bath

2. Where did they go last?

    hall   yard   Peggy's bedroom

3. When did they go to Randy's bedroom?

    first   second   third

4. After the kitchen, where did they go next?

    yard   Mom's bedroom   bath

5. After Mom and Dad's bedroom, where did they look next?

    kitchen   yard   Peggy's bedroom

This is a lily pad.
It grows in a pond.

This is a pink lily flower.
It grows on the lily pad.

Mr. Frog sits in the middle
of a lily pad. He sits with
his eyes shut.

Some little green bugs came flying to Pink Lily Pond.

Van Bug called, "See that old, fat frog sleeping in the middle of the pond."

"Let's zoom down and tickle him," said Belle Bug. "Old, fat frogs are not quick."

So all the little green bugs zoomed down to tickle Mr. Frog. They were careful to tickle his back. What fun they had! They laughed until their wings shook! Tickle! Tickle! Tickle!

Some bugs forgot and went too near Mr. Frog's mouth. Surprise! Out came a long tongue! Zap! Zap! The bugs were stuck on that sticky tongue.

Surprise! The sticky tongue rolled back into Mr. Frog's mouth! Mr. Frog's eyes were open now! He had fooled the bugs. He was happy! What a good lunch he was having!

Van Bug said, "So, Belle, never think an old, fat frog cannot be fast! It may fool you!"

A **Which one is right? Put a ✓ by it.**

1. Where did Mr. Frog sit?

_____ a. on a lily pad

_____ b. on a rock

_____ c. in the water

2. Where were the pink lily flowers growing?

_____ a. in water

_____ b. on land

_____ c. in trees

3. What were the bugs careful to do at first?

_____ a. keep the frog's eyes shut

_____ b. stay near the frog's mouth

_____ c. stay in back of the frog

4. Why didn't the bugs fly off the tongue?

_____ a. They wanted to tickle it.

_____ b. They were stuck.

_____ c. The bugs' wings shook.

5. Why did Mr. Frog shut his eyes?

_____ a. to fool the bugs

_____ b. to keep the sun out

_____ c. to sleep

6. What word means **not open**?

_____ a. shut _____ b. quick _____ c. pad

7. What did Van Bug tell Belle?

_____ a. Just eat lily pads.

_____ b. Frogs are not good to eat.

_____ c. Be careful near **all** frogs.

8. What is the best name for this story?

_____ a. The Bugs Fool Mr. Frog

_____ b. The Pretty Pink Lily Pad

_____ c. Mr. Frog's Trick

B **Draw lines to match these.**

1. play a trick on

2. part of a lily plant

3. fast

4. could not get out

5. put your teeth into

6. part of a mouth

7. makes you feel funny

pad

quick

open

tongue

bite

fool

stuck

tickle

A dictionary tells you what a word means.
Words in a dictionary are put in ABC order.

eyes The eyes help us see.

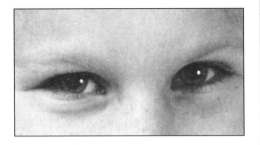

hands The hands help us pick up things.

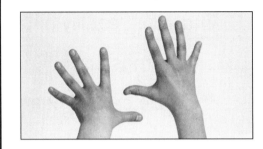

feet We walk and run on our feet.

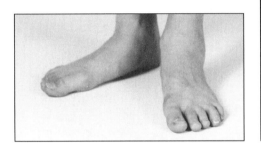

mouth My teeth are in my mouth.

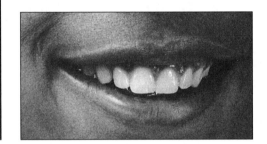

Write the words from the picture dictionary above.

1. What helps us hold this book? _____

2. What helps us look at TV? _____

3. If the word **nose** were on this page, where would it go? Put a ✔ by the right answer.

   _____ a. after **mouth**

   _____ b. before **mouth**

   _____ c. before **eyes**

Nicky said, "I'm going to Sam's birthday party next Sunday."

"How old will Sam be?" asked Nicky's big sister, Donna.

"Seven," said Nicky. "His dad made him a cake with seven candles on it."

Nicky told Donna more about the party. "Sam's a big boy now! So his mother let him buy things for the party. Sam asked seven friends to the party. He went out to buy seven funny hats, seven balloons, and seven games for his friends."

"Oh, oh," said Donna. "I think someone will not be happy at Sam's party. He did not buy enough hats, balloons, and games for his friends."

"Yes, he did!" said Nicky.

Then he counted. "Sam asked Ann, Carmen, and Dolly. He asked Tim, Carlos, José, and me. That makes seven of us."

Donna said nothing.

Sunday evening Nicky came home. He yelled, "You were right, Donna. Sam did not have enough hats, balloons, and games. How did you know what would happen?"

His sister said, "If you think, you can work it out, too."

Think like Donna. What did Sam forget? How many balloons, games, and hats did he need?

A **Which one is right? Put a ✔ by it.**

1. How many girls did Sam ask to the party?

_____ a. four _____ b. three _____ c. no girls

2. How many funny hats did Sam need?

_____ a. eight _____ b. seven _____ c. nine

3. When did Donna know Sam forgot something?

_____ a. before the party

_____ b. after the party

_____ c. before Sam got the hats

4. What did Sam forget?

_____ a. to count the people he asked

_____ b. to count himself

_____ c. to count the girls

5. What do you think happened at Sam's party?

_____ a. Every child got a funny hat.

_____ b. There were too many funny hats.

_____ c. One child did not get a funny hat.

6. What is the best name for this story?

_____ a. A Good Party

_____ b. Sam Forgets Something

_____ c. Donna Forgets Something

B **Draw lines to match these.**

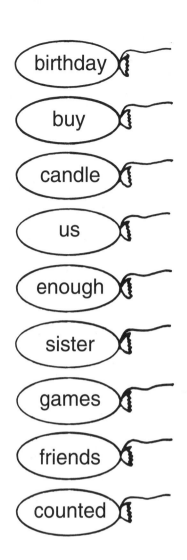

birthday

buy

candle

us

enough

sister

games

friends

counted

1. girl in the family

2. day you were born

3. as many as you need

4. to get things with money

5. people you like

6. something that gives light

7. you and me

8. said, "One, two, three, . . ."

 Draw lines to put the first part of the sentence with the last part.

1. Every year people

2. Birthdays come

3. We have fun with

4. Candles are put

5. People count to find out

6. We eat cake

7. Evening comes

a. one time a year.

b. how many there are.

c. on top of cakes.

d. get older.

e. before night.

f. games and balloons.

g. on a funny hat.

h. after dinner.

69

D **Circle the best way to end each story.**

1. It is Carmen's birthday. She is four now. She will be five years old on _____.

   her next birthday   in two years

   her last birthday   last week

2. Sam did not eat all of the cake. He ate the top of it. He ate the middle. He did not eat the _____.

   middle   bottom   count

3. Nicky counted the books. There were eight books. Then he counted the children. He counted nine children.

   Nicky did not have _____.

   every   each   enough

4. Donna got a new plant for her birthday. It was in a red flower pot. The pot had a hole in the bottom. Donna put too much water into the pot. Some of the water came out of the _____.

   flower   hole   birthday

5. One night the lights went out. José and Carmen could not see in the house. Mother found something that makes light. Mother found some _____.

   counts   enough   candles

Baby Tiger walked next to his mother all the time. He was afraid of other animals. He began to cry.

Mother Tiger said, "Do not be afraid of other animals, Baby Tiger. Other animals are afraid of us."

Other animals walked by. They looked at the two tigers. They stayed far away from the tigers.

One evening, Mother Tiger was sleeping. Baby Tiger went for a walk alone. He smelled something by a big rock. Baby Tiger looked in back of the rock. He saw an animal that he had never seen before.

The animal looked at Baby Tiger. It went "S—s—s—s—s!" at him.

Baby Tiger said, "You are a funny animal. You have no feet. You have no ears. You are very, very long!"

The funny animal had no feet, but it could move fast. It was quick. Zip! It was all around Baby Tiger. Baby Tiger began to cry.

Mother Tiger came running to help Baby Tiger. Zip! The funny animal went away fast.

Mother Tiger said, "Do not go near that animal again. It can't eat you, but it can bite you!"

A Which one is right? Put a ✓ by it.

1. What happened first?

   _____ a. Baby Tiger looked in back of a rock.

   _____ b. Baby Tiger talked to the other animal.

   _____ c. Baby Tiger smelled something.

2. What animal do you think Baby Tiger saw?

   _____ a. bee _____ b. snake _____ c. worm

3. Why do other animals stay away from tigers?

   _____ a. Tigers do not smell good.

   _____ b. Tigers are afraid of other animals.

   _____ c. Tigers can eat other animals.

4. When did this story happen?

   _____ a. morning _____ b. noon _____ c. evening

5. What can the funny animal do to tigers?

   _____ a. bite them

   _____ b. eat them

   _____ c. play with them

6. What did we learn from this story?

   _____ a. Baby tigers can learn to sleep.

   _____ b. Baby animals learn from their mothers.

   _____ c. Baby animals are never afraid.

7. What is the best name for this story?

_____ a. Baby Tiger Learns Something New

_____ b. Baby Tiger and the Bees

_____ c. Tigers Are Never Afraid

B **Put a word from the box into each sentence.**

began	snake	bite	other
afraid	quick	smell	around

1. The _____ hid under a rock.

2. Snakes eat _____ animals.

3. Many animals are _____ of tigers.

4. A snake can _____ a tiger.

5. A skunk may let out a bad _____.

C **Read this story. Tell when each one walked by. Put 1, 2, 3, and 4 under the pictures.**

First, a skunk walked by the tigers. Next, a fox ran by them. Then, a frog hopped by the tigers. Last, a duck walked by them.

_____   _____   _____   _____

Find the best name for each story. Put the letter of the name on the line.

Names
a. Land and Water Animals
b. The Giant Falls
c. The Giant Wants To Ride
d. Air Is Near Us
e. Air Can Go Fast
f. Animals at the Zoo

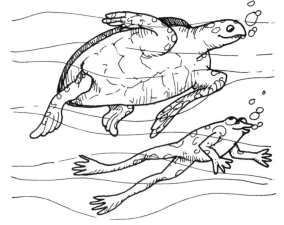

_____ **Story 1**

Air is all around us. You cannot see it or smell it. But air is there. All plants and animals must have air to live.

_____ **Story 2**

Frogs and turtles can live in the water. But they can live on land, too. Animals that live on land and in the water can walk and swim. Can ducks and seals do this?

_____ **Story 3**

Sometimes air moves very fast. It makes a wind. The wind can blow things away. It can make kites fly. The fast air makes sailboats go.

_____ **Story 4**

Mr. Giant of Pink Lily Pond went to look for a friend. He walked far from the pond. He did not look where he was going. His feet walked right into a tall building. Mr. Giant fell down on top of a big city!

On Monday, Helene did not want to eat her cake. She left it on the picnic table and went to play. When she came back, the cake was gone!

"Who took my cake?" said Helene to her sister and brothers.

"I didn't!" said Judy, Mike, and Ben.

Tuesday afternoon, Judy left an orange on the picnic table. When she came back, the orange was gone!

On Wednesday, Mike put bread on the table for lunch. When he went to get more food, someone took the bread.

It happened again on Thursday! Someone took Ben's apple!

Helene wanted to find out who was taking the food. On Friday, she put some candy on the picnic table. Then she hid around the corner of the house. She could not see the table, but

she
could
see
its

Helene saw Judy go by. Then she saw Mike and Ben go by. The candy was still there. Then Helene saw this.

A **Which one is right? Put a ✔ by it.**

1. What was this story about?

_____ a. a girl who could think

_____ b. a cat who took food

_____ c. a boy who took food

2. What foods were taken?

_____ a. bread, butter, lettuce, cake

_____ b. eggs, lettuce, orange, candy

_____ c. apple, cake, bread, orange

3. What do we know about the day that Helene hid?

_____ a. It was a hot day.

_____ b. There was no sun that day.

_____ c. The sun was out.

4. Who took the food?

_____ a. a squirrel _____ b. Judy _____ c. Ben

5. Where did Helene hide?

_____ a. under the table in the yard

_____ b. in a tree by the table

_____ c. around the corner of the house

6. When did someone take Ben's apple?

_____ a. Wednesday _____ b. Thursday _____ c. Friday

7. What did Helene see first?

   _____ a. her sister and brothers

   _____ b. her father and mother

   _____ c. a squirrel

8. What is the best name for this story?

   _____ a. Mike and the Lost Food

   _____ b. Who Took the Food?

   _____ c. Ben Takes the Candy

B **Write the name of each thing next to the picture.**
Then tell which day each thing was taken.

apple	bread	candy	cake	orange
Thursday	Tuesday	Wednesday	Friday	Monday

                     Food   **Day**

1. _____ _____

2. _____ _____

3. _____ _____

4. _____ _____

5. _____ _____

What was left on the table? Find a sentence that tells. Put the letter of the sentence by the right table.

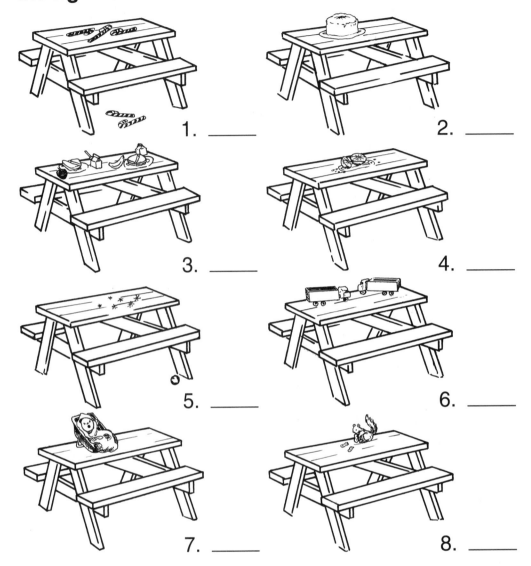

1. _____

2. _____

3. _____

4. _____

5. _____

6. _____

7. _____

8. _____

a. We put a cake on the table to cool.

b. Dad left some coats and hats on the table.

c. Something is here, but the ball rolled off.

d. Some of the candy has fallen on the ground.

e. The squirrel is eating nuts on the table.

f. The baby is not happy on the table.

g. The chairs are on top of the table.

h. We left our toy trucks on the table.

i. Our lunch is ready to eat on the table.

j. This orange has many seeds inside.

Read the stories. Follow the directions.

1. Tilly, Milly, Billy, and Jilly lost their
   mittens. They looked and looked. They found
   nine mittens. What do we know about
   the mittens now? Circle <u>two</u> right answers.

   a. There were not enough mittens.

   b. There were four green mittens.

   c. There were enough mittens.

   d. There was one mitten left over.

2. Five children were in line. Jay was first.
   May was last. Fay was second. Ray was next to
   last. Where was Kay? Circle <u>two</u> right answers.

   a. Kay was second.

   b. Kay was in the middle.

   c. Kay was third.

   d. Kay was last.

3. Dan got something in the middle store. Nan got
   something in the first store. Van got something in the
   last store. Fran got something in the second store.
   What did the children get? Circle <u>three</u> right answers.

   a. Fran got a book.   b. Jan got some pizza.

   c. Nan got a doll.   d. Van got his hair cut.

B **Follow the tiger's tracks. Can you tell where the tiger went? Put a ✔ by the right words.**

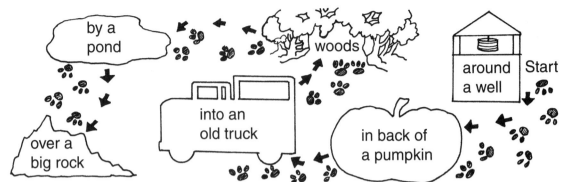

1. Where did the tiger go first?

    _____ a. around a well

    _____ b. in back of a pumpkin

2. Where did the tiger go last?

    _____ a. into the woods

    _____ b. over a big rock

3. Where was the tiger before it got to the pond?

    _____ a. in the woods

    _____ b. at the big rock

4. Where did the tiger go when it left the well?

    _____ a. over the water

    _____ b. in back of the pumpkin

5. When did the tiger get to the old truck?

    _____ a. before it got to the trees

    _____ b. after it got to the trees

C **Here is a page from a picture dictionary. The words are in ABC order.**

banana   A banana is long and yellow.

carrot   A carrot is long and orange.

doughnut   A doughnut is sweet and good to eat.

egg   An egg is white or brown.

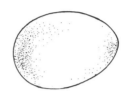

Write the words from the picture dictionary above.

1. What food sometimes has a hole in the middle?

   _____

2. What food is picked from trees? _____

3. If you had to put the words **onion** and **fig** on this dictionary page, which word would come first?

   Write the word. _____

4. If you want to put the word **apple** on this page, where would it go? Circle the right answer.

   after **egg**   after **carrot**   before **banana**   81

D Here is the Table of Contents page of a book. Use it to answer the questions. Circle the right answer.

Stories

The Pink Candle 2

The Sticky Mud 5

A Worm Tickles Robin 7

Care of Your Teeth 10

A Rainy Day 15

1. On which page will you find *Care of Your Teeth*?

   a. 10   b. 7   c. 15

2. How many stories are in this book?

   a. 4   b. 5   c. 10

3. Which story starts on page 7?

   a. last one   b. first one   c. middle one

4. Which story is the last one?
   a. *The Pink Candle*
   b. *A Rainy Day*
   c. *The Sticky Mud*

5. Which story is about a light?
   a. *A Worm Tickles Robin*
   b. *Care of Your Teeth*
   c. *The Pink Candle*

E **Draw lines to put the first part of the sentence with the last part.**

1. A frog's tongue is   a. of tigers.

2. Rain makes   b. the sand wet.

3. We watch TV in   c. the baby will cry.

4. Some animals are afraid d. long and sticky.

5. If you tickle me,   e. I will laugh.

6. Snakes have no   f. the living room.

                           g. hands and feet.

F **Fun time! Guess who? Write the name of the animal next to its picture.**

ant   fish   rabbit   seal
snake   squirrel   skunk   tiger

1.  _____

2.  _____

3.  _____

4. _____

5. _____

Do any of the police officers in your city ride horses? Some cities do have mounted police. One of these cities is Baltimore, Maryland.

A soldier started the horse police in Baltimore many years ago. Now there are more of them because horses can get out of traffic jams better than police cars.

For many years the most popular police horse was a big brown horse with a black mane named Mike. When Mike went to work for the city, he was a little wild. Mike stood up on his hind legs and the rider slid off. Police Officer Bob was the only one strong enough to stay on Mike's back. Even he was sometimes thrown off and landed in the street.

After sliding off Mike several times, Bob got tired of landing on his back in the street with everyone laughing. So Bob learned to hold on tightly to the reins with both hands. That way he could control tricky Mike better.

After a time the big horse became as gentle as a lamb. Bob, on top of Mike, directed traffic, rode in parades, and posed for thousands of pictures people took. Children often came up to feed apples or carrots to the horse they loved.

On streets where houses came up to the sidewalk, Bob often rode Mike right up to the windows to see sick people. The people could come to the window and pat Mike on his nose. It made them happy to have the horse visit.

But Bob and Mike had hard jobs, too. They galloped down back streets and cut off racing bank robbers. If there were fights, the police officer and horse could break them up.

Mike had good care. He lived in a nice stall. He had people to wash him, brush his mane, and feed him. A vet came when he was sick. A blacksmith put new horseshoes on Mike whenever he needed them.

Now Mike is too old to work. Bob has found him a home on a farm. Of course, Bob comes to visit his four-legged friend often.

 Read the words in the Word Box. Write the correct words next to the meanings.

Word Box	popular	reins	hind
	wild	mane	gallop
	mounted	gentle	stall

1. liked by many people   _____

2. place where a horse sleeps   _____

3. back legs   _____

4. opposite of wild   _____

5. got up on a horse   _____

6. hair on a horse's neck   _____

7. ride very quickly   _____

8. hard to control   _____

B <u>Underline</u> **the right answer.**

1. What is this story mainly about?

    a. how people train wild horses

    b. how a vet and a blacksmith take care of horses

    c. how a man and an animal worked together

2. When did the wild horse become as gentle as a lamb?

    a. before Bob fell in the street

    b. after Bob could control him

    c. before people laughed at Bob

3. How do horses help the police?

    a. They carry food for them.

    b. They help the police keep traffic moving.

    c. They bring doctors to sick people.

4. What is another job Bob and Mike did?

    a. They rode in parades.

    b. They ran after runaway cows.

    c. They took money to banks.

5. How do we know the horse was popular with children?

    a. Someone made up a song about him.

    b. Children got new reins for the horse.

    c. Children took food to him.

6. Who takes care of sick horses?

    a. a vet

    b. a blacksmith

    c. people who are ill

7. How did Bob teach Mike not to be wild?

    a. He told him to be gentle.

    b. He controlled him with the reins.

    c. He took him to the vet.

Draw a line from each sentence to the right picture.
One is done for you.

a.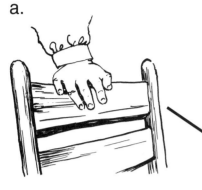

b.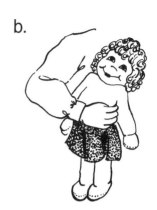

1. Hand the toy to me.
2. Put your hand on the chair.

c.

d.

3. He leaves the stall.
4. The leaves are green.

e.

f.

5. The rock is large.
6. See the chair rock.

g.

h.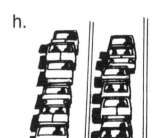

7. It is hard to move in a traffic jam.
8. Put some jam on the bread.

i.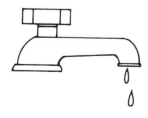

j.

9. She drops the book.
10. Drops of water came out.

Here is Mike. Label each part on the animal. Use one word from each pair of words.

Labels		
mane, man	run, reins	not, nose
mount, mouth	tail, tall	legs, leaves
saddle, stall	ears, hears	

1. _____

2. _____

3. _____

4. _____

5. _____

6. _____

7. _____

8. _____

 Read the stories. Pick the right title that tells the main idea of each story from the box. Write it on the line over the story.

Titles
a. Who Started the Mounted Police
b. How the Mounted Police Are Trained
c. What Mounted Police Wore

1. _____

The mounted police officers wore dark blue riding pants with black boots. Their helmets were white and gold. Their jackets were dark blue and yellow.

2. _____

Police officers who are picked to work with horses must be trained. First, they learn to feed and brush their horses. Then they learn to take care of everything the horse must have on. The officers also learn how to ride in traffic and on city streets.

F <u>Underline</u> the sentence which best tells about each picture.

1.

    a. Bob holds the reins.

    b. Bob dropped the reins.

    c. The reins are on the horse's feet.

2.

    a. The horse stands still.

    b. The horse is in his stall.

    c. The horse is galloping.

3.

    a. The animal controls the person.

    b. The woman controls the traffic.

    c. The woman controls the animal.

4.

    a. The horse's mane is not long.

    b. The mane is on the animal's neck.

    c. The man is doing his job.

5.

    a. She mounted the horse.

    b. She was gentle with her pets.

    c. She was galloping wildly.

Anita was eight years old. Her little brother Gilbert was only three, but he wanted to do everything Anita did. He wanted to go everywhere she went.

Anita had her own secret place. It was a tiny room on the third floor of her house. It was the only place Anita could go to get away from Gilbert. She often heard Gilbert calling her when she was in her room. But he could never find her.

On a warm Thursday in April, Anita opened the window of her room. She forgot to shut it when she left. The next day, she found two birds building a neat little nest on the window sill.

Anita stood very still. She did not make a sound. The birds looked at her, and she looked at them. Soon the birds trusted Anita, so they kept on with their building.

Day after day, Anita saw these wonderful sights.

Three Weeks Later

The three baby birds chirped and called. Their bills were always open. Their parents had to work hard to feed them. Anita was always quiet and still so she would not frighten the hard-working parents or their babies.

"The birds need help," thought Anita. She got these things for her feathered friends.

Just as the sun was coming up, Anita was in the kitchen. She put all these things into a small bowl with some water. She mashed them with a fork. Now she had some soft food for the birds.

Later that day, Anita put a tiny bit of mashed food into each chirping baby bird's mouth. They loved it! They cried for more!

Every day after that Anita fed the baby birds. One day when she was in her secret room, Gilbert found her. He followed her in. "Quiet, Shhh!" Anita whispered.

They tiptoed out of the room. Gilbert didn't want to leave. He wanted to feed the baby birds, too.

"No, you're too little," said Anita.

Gilbert started to cry. Anita didn't want their parents to find out she was feeding the birds. She had to give in to Gilbert.

Gilbert was as quiet as a mouse. He watched his sister put a tiny bit of food into one baby bird's mouth. Then Anita put some food on Gilbert's little finger. She held him while he fed some mashed food to one of the birds.

The baby bird was hungry. It ate all the food. Gilbert was excited, but he stayed very quiet.

That is, Gilbert was quiet until he and Anita got downstairs. Then he rushed to his mother and father shouting,

"I'm a mother! I'm a mother! I can feed baby birds!"

Underline the right answers.

1. Where did the birds make their nest?

   a. on a tree

   b. on a window sill

   c. by a big rock

2. What did Anita mash for food?

   a. bread, seeds, and cereal

   b. cereal, seeds, and pizza

   c. flowers, seeds, and bread

3. When did this story happen?

   a. when it was very cold

   b. one warm spring day

   c. on a very rainy day

4. Why did Gilbert say, "I am a mother!"?

   a. He told Anita what to do.

   b. He knew how to be quiet.

   c. He thought mothers always fed babies.

5. What did Gilbert do to be quiet?

   a. He turned off the TV.

   b. He put his hand over his mouth.

   c. He locked the door.

6. How did Gilbert find out about the birds?

   a. He saw some feathers.

   b. He followed Anita.

   c. He heard the birds sing.

7. What is the best name for this story?

   a. A Room with a Lock

   b. Dad Feeds the Birds

   c. Gilbert and Anita Make New Friends

Detective Sharp Eye says, "If you find it hard to answer a question, always look back in the story. Read it again. Write your answers on the blank lines."

1. When did Anita forget to shut the window?

    a. What day was it? _____

    b. What month was it? _____

    c. Was it warm or cold? _____

    d. Now here is a thought question. Why do you think Anita forgot to shut the window?

    _____

    _____

2. The next day Anita went back to her secret room.

    a. What day would that be? _____

    b. What did she find there? _____

    c. Where were the birds? _____

3. Day after day, Anita saw wonderful sights.

    a. How many eggs did the birds lay? _____

    b. How long did it take for babies to come out of

        the eggs? _____

4. When did Anita make baby bird food?

    _____

    _____

    _____

a. What is that part of the day? Circle the right one.

afternoon   morning   evening

b. Why did she make the food at that time?

_____

_____

5. Where was the secret room? Circle the right one.

a. second floor   b. first floor   c. third floor

What do you think happened after Gilbert told their parents what he and Anita had been doing? Read these endings. Put a ✔ by the ones you think could happen. Put an X by the ones that you think did not happen.

_____ 1. The family ate bird food for dinner.

_____ 2. Mom moved the birds and nest into the kitchen.

_____ 3. Mom and Dad went to see the nest.

_____ 4. The parents let the children keep on feeding the babies.

_____ 5. The birds learned to talk.

_____ 6. The birds gave food to Anita and Gilbert.

_____ 7. Gilbert frightened the birds away.

_____ 8. The baby birds got bigger and bigger.

_____ 9. Anita learned to trust her little brother.

_____ 10. The door of the secret room was locked, and the children never went in again.

D **Write the word that goes with the meaning in each egg.**

a. secret
b. wonderful
c. lock
d. quiet
e. always
f. building
g. frighten
h. hungry
i. shut

part of a door

every time

1. _____

2. _____

something one
person knows

to close

3. _____

4. _____

needs food

very, very good

5. _____

6. _____

not noisy

to scare

7. _____

8. _____

95

On Tuesday, some of Daisy's classmates asked, "Did you bring your check?"

"What check?" asked Daisy.

It was time to get back to work. No one had time to answer Daisy.

On the way home that afternoon, Daisy met her friend, Detective Sharp Eye. Daisy began to cry as she told him that she needed a check.

"What kind of check?" asked the detective.

Daisy whispered, "I don't know. I didn't understand."

"Let's try this check," said Mr. Sharp Eye. He gave Daisy a piece of pink paper. He made a big ✔ on it.

On Wednesday morning, Daisy was happy when she gave the teacher the check. Ms. Boone was not happy!

On the way home, Daisy met Detective Sharp Eye again.

"Let's see what kind of check Ms. Boone wants," he said. "We know it is not a check like the one on the pink paper. Do you think it is a check like the ones on my cap? Or, can it be some checkers?"

Daisy didn't know, so they went to ask Ms. Boone.

Ms. Boone looked surprised. "Daisy, you need a check to pay for the trip to see the pandas," she said.

"Now we understand," said Detective Sharp Eye. "When we talk about checks, we must know what kind of check is needed."

This is the check Daisy's mom gave her.

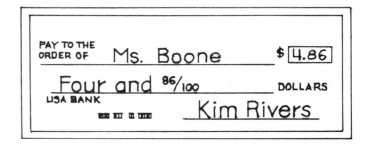

A **Underline the right answer.**

1. Why did Daisy cry?

    a. She had too many checks.

    b. She lost her check.

    c. She didn't have a check.

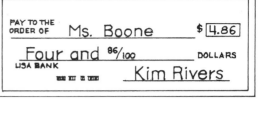

2. What is this story about?

    a. a girl who did not see the pandas

    b. a girl who lost something

    c. a girl who didn't understand

3. Why did Daisy need help?

    a. Her mother did not have any checks.

    b. She did not know what kind of check to get.

    c. She always tripped.

4. Who was trying to help Daisy?

    a. a girl in her class

    b. a boy in her class

    c. a detective

5. What happened first?

    a. Daisy's check on pink paper

    b. the trip to see the pandas

    c. the check Daisy's mother gave her

6. Why did the class need the checks?

    a. to see if their work was good

    b. to pay for a trip to the zoo

    c. to get new caps

7. What was Detective Sharp Eye trying to teach Daisy?

    a. Words must be spelled right.

    b. She could not understand Ms. Boone's words.

    c. A word can have many meanings.

8. What surprised Ms. Boone about Daisy?

    a. that Daisy was Detective Sharp Eye's friend

    b. that Daisy did not know about the check

    c. that Daisy had checks on her coat

 Detective Sharp Eye says, "Words can have many meanings." Draw a line from the picture to the correct sentence.

1.   a. They have checked pants.

2.    b. He checks a number in the telephone book.

3.    c. She checks the children's work.

4.    d. They play checkers.

5.    e. She pays with a check.

98

Detective Sharp Eye says, "If you read carefully, you can tell who wrote these letters. Good luck!" Write the name from the box under the letter.

Ms. Boone	Pam Panda
Mr. Sharp Eye	Daisy Rivers

1. Dear Mrs. Rivers,

   Last week I met Daisy after school. She needed help again. She couldn't find her homework. I told her to think about all of the places she had been that day. She did find her homework that way. Someday she will be a good detective, too.

   Your friend,

   _____

2. Dear Mrs. Rivers,

   Daisy has been working very hard. She did very well on her math test.

   She told the class all about pandas when we went to the zoo. The class learned a lot from her.

   I hope Daisy keeps up the good work.

   Yours,

   _____

3. Dear Mr. Zookeeper,

   Why are all these people looking at us? They talk to us. They want to feed us. They will not let us sleep. If this keeps up, we will hide every day during visiting hours.

   Yours,

   _____

D (Circle) **the letter of the right meaning for each underlined word.**

1. Daisy's <u>classmates</u> knew about the trip.

   a. brothers and sisters

   b. the children in her room at school

   c. the children in the city

2. Daisy was afraid that she would <u>trip</u>.

   a. go away　　　b. forget　　　c. fall

3. The class took a <u>trip</u>.

   a. fell down

   b. checked their work

   c. went somewhere

4. Mr. Sharp Eye <u>forgot</u> his lunch.

   a. took it home

   b. ate all of it

   c. did not remember to bring it

5. Mother <u>needed</u> a new checkbook.

   a. had to have　　　b. did not want　　　c. had to go away

6. "Did you bring the check?" <u>questioned</u> the teacher.

   a. asked　　　b. answered　　　c. laughed

E (Circle) **the best name for each story.**

1. One evening, a man came to the door. He had long whiskers and he talked funny. The children were afraid of him. They did not let him into the house. The man laughed and took off the whiskers. It was only Uncle Billy trying to be funny.

   a. The Funny Whiskers

   b. The Funny Whispers

   c. The Sad Woman

2. Our teacher, Miss Blue, always knows what we are doing. She seems to know what we are thinking, too! One day, I was mad at Tommy. I didn't tell anyone, but Miss Blue knew. She said, "Stay after school and help me. That will be better than fighting."

    a. Miss Blue Forgets Something

    b. Tommy Stops a Fight

    c. How Did She Know?

3. Sue was at the pond. A big bee buzzed around her. Sue ran away. The bee flew after her. It swooped down onto Sue's nose. Sue stood very still. She was afraid.

    a. A New Friend

    b. A Bee Lands on a Flower

    c. A Bee Lands on a Nose

F **Detective Sharp Eye says, "If you understand all the words in a sentence, you will know what the sentence means." Underline the sentence that has the closest meaning to the first one.**

1. The child gave the teacher a check.

    a. The child gave the teacher flowers.

    b. The child gave the teacher money.

    c. The child gave the teacher nothing.

2. Daisy and her class took a trip.

    a. They went away.

    b. They fell down.

    c. Daisy fell down.

3. Daisy followed her friends.

    a. She walked after them.

    b. She walked before them.

    c. She went the other way.

One Thursday evening in May, Ann and Jeff had a cookout in their front yard. Jeff asked three of his friends to come. Ann asked four children from her class to come.

The cookout started at five o'clock. Dad cooked hot dogs and hamburgers over a grill. Mom cooked potatoes and corn, too. The children ate until they were full!

"Now it is time for the treasure hunt!" Ann yelled.

"The one who finds the treasure box can keep it!"

Jeff led the children to the side yard. They hunted for the treasure box. No one found it.

They ran on to the back yard. Ann's friend, Ed, found the treasure box. It was hidden between two rocks near the oak tree.

The treasure box was full of tiny toys for everyone to take home. The girls picked out small red, white, and blue drums. The boys wanted the little orange horns. Ed got to keep the treasure box and a horn.

Then Mom had a big surprise! She had little ice creams in the shape of flowers for everyone. At seven o'clock the children finished eating their ice cream and went home.

Underline the right answer.

1. What was this story about?

    a. cooking out on the sand

    b. a cookout at someone's house

    c. a cookout at school

2. Which food did they eat at the cookout?

    a. cake   b. corn   c. candy

3. How many boys were at this cookout?

    a. four

    b. five

    c. The story did not tell.

4. Where did the children hunt first?

    a. in the side yard

    b. in the back yard

    c. The story did not tell.

5. When did they eat ice cream?

    a. before seven o'clock

    b. before five o'clock

    c. after seven o'clock

6. Where was the treasure box?

    a. between some rocks

    b. under some rocks

    c. up in an oak tree

7. Which treasure do you think Mary got?

    a. a drum   b. a horn   c. a treasure box

8. What is the best name for this story?

    a. A Day of Fun

    b. An Evening of Fun

    c. The Picnic in the Park

B

Dear Friends,

    Be a smart detective like me. Here are some hard questions. Put your clues together and solve the mystery. Good luck!

                               Detective Sharp Eye

1. How many children were at the cookout? Use these steps and your story to find out.

    a. First, circle the faces of the children who gave the cookout.

       How many did you circle? _____

    b. Next, check off the number of children Jeff asked to the cookout. How many did Jeff ask? _____

    c. Now check off the number of children Ann asked to the cookout. How many did Ann ask? _____

    d. Cross out any faces you did not need.

    e. Now add the numbers to tell how many children were at the cookout. _____ children were there.

2. How long did the cookout last? Look for clues in the story. Here is how Detective Sharp Eye worked it out!

    a. Tell the time the cookout started. _____

    b. Tell the time the cookout ended. _____

    c. Now you can tell how long the cookout lasted. _____ hours

104

3. Ed found the treasure box. Which child is sharp-eyed Ed? Read the clues about these three boys to find out.

_____   _____   _____

     Jeff is a tall boy who likes to play ball. He has asked his friends to the cookout.

     Ed likes to play baseball. Ed's team always plays on Thursday afternoons.

     Tommy likes to play ball games with Ed and Jeff. Tommy is not a tall boy. He is shorter than Jeff and Ed.

  a. Write each boy's name under his picture.

  b. Put a big box around Ed's picture.

4. What did the children eat at the cookout? Look in the story. Can you tell every food they ate?

_____   _____

_____   _____

_____

5. Did the children like the food? Write the sentence from the story which tells if the children liked the food.

_____

6. Where were the hot dogs cooked? They were cooked on a

_____ .

7. What did the ice cream look like?

Write the word. _____
Use the space at the right to draw
the shape of the ice cream they ate.

C **Can you put the right word in each sentence?**

| treasure | cookout | class | shape |
| hamburger | between | grill | potato |

1. A _____ is a meal fixed outdoors.

2. They cut the brown skin off the white _____.

3. Some ground meat on a roll is called a _____.

4. We use a _____ to cook meat over a fire.

5. A very good thing that everyone wants is a _____.

6. The ice cream was cut in the _____ of flowers.

7. Children in Jeff's room at school are in his _____.

D **Circle the right word to end the sentence.**

1. Father made a fire. Then he put the hot dogs on the _____ to cook.

   a. ground   b. grill   c. grass

2. The hamburgers were ready to eat. They smelled so good. Each child put a hamburger on a _____.

   a. rug   b. rock   c. roll

3. Ed looked near the oak tree. He found a box. He opened it and found a _____ in it.

   a. treetop   b. treasure   c. through

4. Ed found the treasure _____ two big rocks.

   a. between   b. belong   c. became

5. Ann asked some friends in her _____ to the cookout.

   a. class   b. climb   c. clock

6. The sun goes down and it gets dark in the _____.

   a. every   b. even   c. evening

7. The hamburger rolls were the same _____ as the meat.

   a. shake   b. shape   c. shell

Let's have a treasure hunt. Ed found the treasure. Follow his tracks and find the treasure. Can you answer the questions?

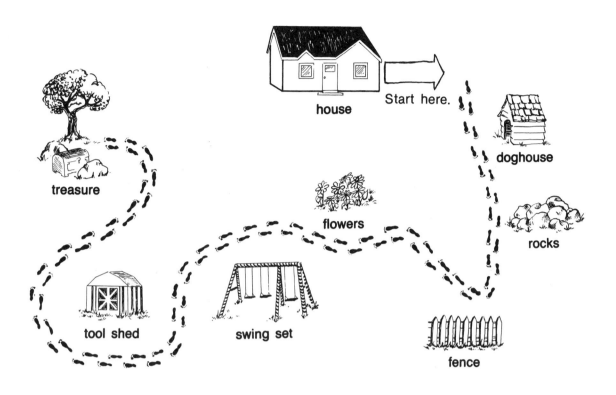

1. Where did Ed start out? _____

2. Where did he find the treasure? _____

3. Where did Ed go after he left the house? _____

4. Where did he go just before he got to the flowers? _____

   _____

5. Where did he go between the fence and the swing set? _____

   _____

6. Where was the fifth place Ed went? _____

7. Where was the third place Ed went? _____

8. Where did Ed go before he went to the fence? _____

9. Where would you hide the treasure? _____

10. Put an **X** on the place where Ed found the treasure.

1 Lee played on the beach one morning. He walked near the water. His feet felt wet and cold, but it was a hot July day.

2 The sea came up on the sand. It splashed on Lee's feet. Then the water went back out again. Every time the sea went out, it left water plants all over the sand. It left many kinds of shells on the sand, too.

3 Lee found some shells and put them in his bag. The sea came splashing up on the sand again. Lee picked up a beautiful pink shell. He had never seen a shell like this one before. Then Lee saw a friend walking over to him.

4 "That is a very pretty shell," said Lee's friend. "That kind of shell is hard to find. If you will sell it to me, I will pay you ten dollars."

5 Lee did not know what to do. He liked the shell, but he wanted the money, too. Then he thought that the sea might bring him another beautiful shell some day soon. Lee sold the shell.

 Underline the right answer.

1. What is this story about?

    a. Lee found something good.

    b. Lee lost something.

    c. A friend found what Lee had lost.

2. When did Lee play on the beach?

    a. one afternoon in June

    b. one July morning

    c. on a May evening

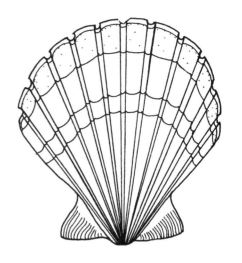

3. Where did this happen?

    a. on a boat

    b. near the sea

    c. in a garden

4. Why were Lee's feet so cold and wet?

    a. The sea was splashing them.

    b. It was raining.

    c. He walked in the pond.

5. What did Lee get for the shell?

    a. ten dollars

    b. nothing

    c. two dollars

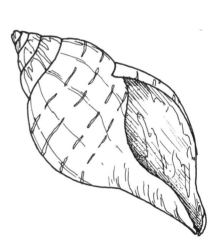

6. Why did Lee's friend want the shell?

    a. It was not like other shells.

    b. The shell had a fish in it.

    c. He wanted to play with it.

7. When did Lee's friend give Lee some money?

    a. before Lee found the shell

    b. after Lee found the shell

    c. He never gave Lee any money.

8. What is the best name for this story?

    a. The Sea Went Out Again

    b. A Sandy Story

    c. Lee Sells Something

B This story has five parts called **paragraphs.** Each paragraph has a number beside it. Detective Sharp Eye wants you to find these things.

1. Write the first word in paragraph **3**. _____

2. Write the third word in paragraph **2**. _____

3. Write the last word in paragraph **5**. _____

4. Write the last word in paragraph **4**. _____

5. Write the second word in paragraph **1**. _____

C Are you a good detective? Write the number of the paragraph that tells:

1. the kind of day it was _____

2. how much money Lee got from his friend _____

3. what Lee picked up _____

4. the color of the shell _____

5. if Lee sold the shell _____

6. what splashed on Lee's feet _____

D What is each paragraph about? Look at the story again. Use the words in the box.

Lee	the sea	a friend

1. Paragraph **1** is about _____.

2. Paragraph **4** is about _____.

3. Paragraph **3** is about _____.

4. Paragraph **5** is about _____.

5. Paragraph **2** is about _____.

110

Which picture goes with the paragraph? Write the letter of the right picture next to the paragraph that tells about it.

1. _____ The sea water splashed up on the sand. It left many things there. It left plants and shells on the sand.

2. _____ Far out on the blue sea was a big boat. The boat was sailing along fast. It was going away from the sand.

3. _____ Some people were walking along the sand. Their feet were getting wet. Other people were swimming and splashing in the deep water.

4. _____ Under the water, many fish were swimming. Some were very big fish. Others were very small. Some fish were swimming together in a school.

5. _____ Then rain started to fall. People came out of the water. Raindrops made the sand wet.

F Use your sharp eyes to find the two sentences in this paragraph that do not belong. Cross them out. Then write the paragraph again. Write only the sentences you did not cross out.

The sea is very big. Many animals live in the sea. Many plants live there, too. A rainbow has many colors. The sea leaves plants and shells on the sand. There are many plants and animals in a forest.

_____

_____

_____

_____

_____

G Write the letter for each word next to the right meaning.

a. dollars   b. thought   c. beautiful   d. morning
e. another   f. splash   g. July   h. every

_____ 1. a summer month   _____ 2. one more

_____ 3. a noise water makes   _____ 4. some money

_____ 5. very pretty   _____ 6. did think

H Find the last part of each sentence. Write the letter of the last part on the line next to the first part of the sentence.

_____ 1. People hunt for shells   a. it must be night.

_____ 2. If you want to buy something,   b. on the sand by the sea.

      c. your feet will get wet.

_____ 3. If it is sunny outside,

_____ 4. If it is dark outside,   d. you must have some money.

_____ 5. If you walk into water,   e. it cannot be night yet.

      f. your feet will not get wet.

How good are your eyes? Look at the picture. Then answer the questions.

1. How many fish can you find in the picture? _____

2. What is all around the plants and animals? _____

3. How many people do you see in the picture? _____

4. How many snakes do you find here? _____

5. How many shells and rocks are there? _____

6. How many times a day must you water these plants? _____

7. Do you see three seals in the picture? _____

8. Are there any rocks in the picture? _____

9. Where is the longest fish swimming?
   (on the top, middle, or bottom) _____

SKILLS REVIEW (Stories 17–21)

 Read this story and answer the questions.

Milly and Ron rode their bikes to the store. They needed to buy some food for lunch. They were very careful on their bikes.

When they got to the store, Ron stayed outside to watch the bikes. Milly went inside the store to buy the food.

Milly looked all around the store for the things she needed. She got bread, hamburger meat, milk, and ice cream. Milly paid for the food and left the store. Then she and Ron rode home.

1. How many paragraphs are in this story? _____

2. Write the last word in the second paragraph. _____

3. Write the sixth word in the third paragraph. _____

4. Write the last word in the first paragraph. _____

5. Write the tenth word in the first paragraph. _____

6. What are the children's names? _____ _____

7. How did the children get to the store? Circle the answer.
   a. They walked.   b. They rode bikes.   c. They took a bus.

8. Why did Ron stay outside the store? Circle the answer.
   a. He watched the bikes.

   b. He could not go inside.

   c. He wanted to stay in the sun.

9. Name all the foods Milly got at the store. _____

_____ _____ _____

10. Paragraph _____ has a sentence that tells when Ron and Milly were going to eat the food.

11. Paragraph _____ tells how careful they were on bikes.

12. Paragraph _____ tells the kinds of food that Milly got.

13. Paragraph _____ is about riding to the store.

14. Paragraph _____ is about buying the food and going home.

15. Paragraph _____ tells who stayed outside the store.

16. The story does not tell us how Ron and Milly carried the food home. But a good detective can learn how they did it. Look back at page 114 for a clue to answer these questions.

   a. How do you think Milly and Ron carried the food home?

   _____

   b. What is the clue that you used? _____

B **Can you write a paragraph? Use four of the sentences below. First, pick the sentence that will start the paragraph. Next, cross out one sentence that does not belong in the paragraph. Last, write your paragraph on the lines below.**

1. They ate hamburgers and then ate ice cream.
2. The children got a letter from Grandmother.
3. Milly and Ron knew how to fix lunch.
4. First, Milly put the bread and plates on the table.
5. Then, Ron cooked the hamburger in a pan.

_____

_____

_____

_____

_____

Detective Sharp Eye wants you to find the picture that goes with each story. Look for clues in the story.

Two children found a treasure. It was a gold horse. The galloping horse had a mane but not reins. Circle the treasure.

1. a.  b.  c.

The two brothers had a small bedroom. One bed was on top of the other bed. The boys liked to sleep in their bunk beds. Find their bedroom. Circle it.

2. a.  b.  c.

The bookworm often stopped in the classroom to take a bite out of the reading books. These books were very sweet and good to eat. One day the bookworm had just taken a bite of a paragraph. A woman came through the door. The woman picked up the book and shut it quickly. Only the bookworm's head was left out of the book. Put a check on the picture that shows what happened.

3. a. 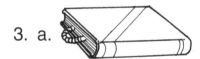 b. 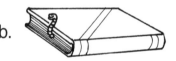 c.

Two girls were sitting at a table. They were playing a game. One girl moved a red circle. The other girl moved a black circle over the top of the red circle. What game were they playing? Circle the game.

4. a. 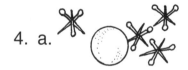 b. 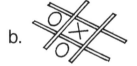 c.

Mrs. Rivers has a new job. She is a mounted police officer. Put a check on her picture.

5. a.  b.  c.

116

D The pandas are in a line. Mark them as the sentences tell you.

1. Circle the second panda.
2. Put an **X** on the middle panda.
3. Underline the third panda and the sixth one.
4. Color the seventh panda yellow.
5. Put a dot on the third panda.
6. Make a star under the fifth and sixth pandas.
7. Put a ✔ over the first and last pandas.

E Draw a line from each sentence to the right picture.

a.

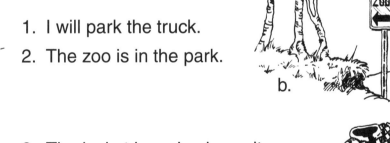

1. I will park the truck.
2. The zoo is in the park.

b.

c.

3. The jacket has checks on it.
4. Daisy put checks on the paper.

d.

5. This is my left hand.
6. We left the car.

e.   f.   **117**

Circle the meaning of the underlined word. Be sure the meaning makes sense.

1. Ms. Boone told Daisy to <u>hand</u> the papers to her classmates.

    a. part of Daisy

    b. give out

    c. take back

2. Jan is the <u>last</u> in line.

    a. the second one

    b. the first one

    c. the end one

3. The boots <u>lasted</u> all winter.

    a. were good for a long time

    b. were not good

    c. were at the end of the line

4. Ricky gave the cat some <u>water</u>.

    a. a place for a boat

    b. something to drink

    c. a brook

G **Fill in the blanks, using the words in the box. Each word may be used more than once.**

light	check	back

1. Please _____ your homework so it will be right.

2. Dan's pants are _____ brown.

3. Ann can pick up the big box. It is _____.

4. Daisy went _____ to school at eleven o'clock.

5. We will write a _____ to pay the bill.

H   **Read each story. Circle the best name.**

1. Two baby birds got bigger. One baby was tiny. The bigger
   babies wanted all the food. Anita saw this. So she always put
   food in the smallest baby's bill. Soon the tiny one got big, too.

   a. Anita Helps a Bird

   b. What Birds Eat

   c. A Bird Helps Anita

2. Two workers took Mike out of his stall. They washed him. They
   brushed his hair. They looked at his horseshoes. Another person
   cleaned Mike's stall.

   a. New Horseshoes

   b. The Horse Gallops

   c. Taking Care of Mike

I   **Write the correct word in each blank.**

rains	reins	checks	mane	main

1. What is the _____ part of the story?

2. When it _____, the streets get wet.

3. She holds the _____ to control the horse.

4. The hair on a horse's neck is a _____.

5. Mom writes _____ to pay the bills.

6. The heavy _____ bring water to the plants.

7. The shirt had red and blue _____ on it.

8. The officer brushed his horse's _____.

9. The rider must hold the horse's _____ to stay on.

(1) Wally Bluewhale was just a baby. But Wally was bigger than a bus! Wally was a whale, and whales are bigger than other animals.

(2) At first, Wally stayed near his mother. They swam together in the sea. Wally had to learn all the things a baby whale must learn. Learning was fun for Wally!

(3) Learning to eat was fun. Mother Bluewhale showed Wally how to open his mouth and swim right through a lot of tiny fish and water plants. As he swam through, the tiny fish and water plants just popped into his mouth. Yum! Yum! Good!

(4) Learning to play was fun, too. Whales cannot stay under water like fish. Whales must go up to the top of the water for air. They made a big game of it. Mother and the other whales splashed out of the water and jumped up in the air! They had fun!

(5) Wally went with them! Bang! His tail hit the water. He liked to hear the noise. He rolled over on his back. He rolled over to his front. He let a big spray of water splash out of his head.

(6) Wally looked at his neighbors in the sea around him. He saw an octopus hiding in the rocks. He saw a big fish eating tiny fish. He saw a turtle hiding in its shell.

(7) "Wow!" said Wally as he rolled over. "I'm so lucky! I'm happy to be me—a big blue whale!"

A **<u>Underline</u> the right answer.**

1. What is one thing we learned about Wally?

   a. He ate big fish.

   b. He was not happy.

   c. He was a happy animal.

2. Why did Wally think he was lucky?

   a. He had to leave the sea.

   b. He found some money in the sea.

   c. He did not have to be afraid of other animals.

3. How do baby whales learn?

   a. by reading a book

   b. by seeing what big whales do

   c. People show them how to do things.

4. Why do whales go to the top of the water?

   a. to play

   b. to eat bugs

   c. to take in air

5. What would happen if Wally did not go to the top of the water?

   a. He would not live.

   b. Nothing would happen.

   c. He would not learn.

6. What can Wally the whale do?

   a. walk on land

   b. sit in a sailboat

   c. spray water from his head

7. What is the best name for this story?

   a. The Lucky Octopus

   b. A Playful Animal

   c. A Careful Animal

B This story has seven paragraphs. Each paragraph has a number before it. Detective Sharp Eye wants you to use the numbers to find these things.

1. Write the first word in paragraph ⑦. _____

2. Write the third word in paragraph ④. _____

3. Write the last word in paragraph ⑦. _____

4. Write the fifth word in paragraph ③. _____

5. Write the eighth word in paragraph ⑤. _____

6. Which paragraph does not have the name *Wally* in it? _____

C Are you a good detective? Which paragraph tells about each of these things? Write the number of the right paragraph in the blank.

_____ 1. whale games

_____ 2. how big Wally was

_____ 3. Wally's food

_____ 4. Wally's neighbors

_____ 5. going up for air

_____ 6. Wally banging his tail

_____ 7. how to eat water plants

_____ 8. how Wally felt about himself

_____ 9. Wally staying near his mother

_____ 10. Wally spraying water from his head

_____ 11. learning to play

_____ 12. what the turtle was doing

D **Can you put the right word in each sentence?**

lucky   learn   through
noise   game   small
hiding   spray   together
      bigger

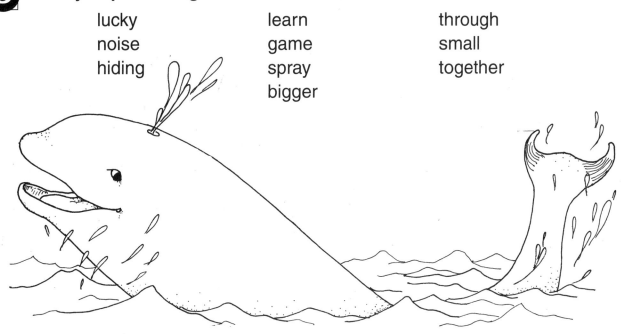

1. Whales can _____ water out of their heads.

2. The big whale swam _____ the water quickly.

3. A baby whale must _____ how to take care of itself.

4. Many fish swimming _____ are called a school of fish.

5. Some fish are so _____ that they are hard to see.

6. Wally said he was _____ to be a big blue whale.

7. Some fish were _____ behind the big rocks in the water.

8. Wally's tail made a lot of _____ when it hit the water.

E **Circle the one word that fits both sentences.**

dish   fish

1. Do you like to hunt and _____?
2. The big _____ stay near the bottom of the pond.

air   are

3. The smell of flowers is in the _____.
4. Open the window and _____ out the room.

Can you write a paragraph? Use four of the sentences below. One sentence does not fit the name of the paragraph. Read the name carefully.

1. Whales are afraid of people.
2. There are many kinds of whales.
3. People kill many whales every year.
4. Whales are not afraid of other animals.
5. Other animals do not kill whales.

What Whales Are Afraid Of

_____

_____

_____

_____

_____

_____

_____

There is a mark at the end of each sentence that means to stop. A sentence that asks you something has a ? at the end. A sentence that tells you something has a . at the end. A sentence that shows that you are mad, happy, or afraid has an ! at the end. Put a . or a ? or an ! at the end of each sentence.

1. Swim fast or they will kill us
2. Did you ever see a whale walking
3. A whale is bigger than a truck
4. Do whales come up to the top of the water for air
5. Wow, I'm so lucky to be me
6. The grass will get green if you spray water on it
7. Help me
8. Is this your lucky day

H **What do you think will happen next? Put a ✔ by it.**

1. Some people were hunting for whales. They were going to kill the whales and sell them. Wally Bluewhale saw the hunters in a boat. What do you think Wally did?

   _____ a. Wally swam into the side of the boat and made the boat go down.

   _____ b. Wally swam far down near the bottom of the sea to hide.

2. Whales swam through the water. They heard a noise and went to see what it was. They came too near land. They got stuck on the land. What do you think happened to the whales?

   _____ a. People had to help the whales get back into the water.

   _____ b. The whales got up and walked back into the water.

3. A baby whale got stuck in an old boat at the bottom of the sea. Baby Whale could not get out. Mother Whale had to help Baby Whale quickly. What did Baby Whale have to do after Mother Whale helped him get out of the old boat?

   _____ a. Baby Whale had to get back in the boat.

   _____ b. Baby Whale had to go up to the top of the water to get some air.

4. The whales had been swimming and playing in the sea. It was time to eat and they were hungry. The whales swam to a place where there were many small fish and water plants. What do you think the whales did?

   _____ a. The whales opened their mouths.

   _____ b. The whales swam to another place in the sea.

23

This was the second time that Jan and Dan were going to camp for two weeks. Last year they had a good time at Camp Oak Tree.

They came to the camp on Saturday morning. Jan and Dan were happy to see their old friends from last year. It was fun to move into the little bunkhouses. They splashed in the lake. Later they ate dinner around the campfire.

Sunday and Monday were beautiful days. Everyone was happy and busy. They played, read, swam, rode horses, and made things.

On Tuesday, things started to happen to make this year different at Camp Oak Tree. It rained hard and long! The bunkhouses had water all over the floors by evening.

The fifth day was sunny. But the children had to mop up the water. They cleaned up the mess until late afternoon.

On Thursday, they went for a long ride on horses. At noon they were ready to eat lunch, but the cook's helpers forgot to bring the food!

The seventh day, some bees came to stay in a tree by the big house. Dan and Jan walked under the tree that morning. The bees buzzed at Dan and stung Jan! But the children still had fun that afternoon going on boat rides on the lake.

On Saturday morning, many people who worked at the camp got sick. They could not take care of the children. That afternoon, fathers and mothers came and took all the children home.

Jan said, "Dan, next year will be better! We'll be back!"

A <u>Underline</u> the right answer.

1. How long did Jan and Dan stay at camp this year?

   a. two weeks   b. one month   c. one week

2. When had Dan and Jan been to camp before?

   a. last month   b. last year   c. last week

3. How did Jan and Dan get home from camp?

   a. They walked home.

   b. Their mother and father came to get them.

   c. They rode in a big bus.

4. What did Dan and Jan do on Wednesday?

   a. They cleaned up the water.

   b. They rode horses all day.

   c. They took boat rides on the lake.

5. Why did water cover the floors of the bunkhouses?

   a. Children forgot to turn the water off.

   b. It rained too much at one time.

   c. The children learned how to swim that way.

6. What came first?

   a. cleaning up the mess

   b. going on boat rides

   c. getting stung by a bee

7. What would have happened if no one had become sick?

   a. The children would have stayed one more day.

   b. The children would have stayed one more month.

   c. The children would have stayed one more week.

8. What is the best name for this story?

   a. Dan and Jan at Camp Oak Tree

   b. Camping Out in the Woods

   c. Bees Come to Camp Oak Tree

Fill in the missing days and times. These lists will help you!

Days of the Week

1. Sunday	5. Thursday
2. Monday	6. Friday
3. Tuesday	7. Saturday
4. Wednesday	

Times of the Day

1. morning	4. evening
2. noon	5. night
3. afternoon	6. midnight

1. Thursday, _____, Saturday

2. Sunday, _____, Tuesday, _____

3. Wednesday, _____, _____

4. _____, Saturday, _____, Monday

5. _____, _____, Thursday

6. noon, afternoon, _____, night

7. _____, noon, afternoon, evening, _____

8. _____, midnight, morning, _____

C **Here is part of a calendar. Can you mark the days when these things happened?**

JULY

Sunday	Monday	Tuesday	Wednesday	Thursday	Friday	Saturday
						7
8	9	10	11	12	13	14
15						

1. Put a purple ✔ on the day the children had to mop up water.
2. Put a green dot on the second day they were at camp.
3. Make a tiny orange box on the day they had to go home.
4. Make a big yellow sun on the day they got to Camp Oak Tree.
5. Put two drops of rain on the day it rained all day.
6. Draw a bee on the day Jan got stung by a bee.
7. Make a circle around the day no one ate lunch.
8. Put a black **M** on the day some people got sick.

When did this happen? A smart detective will check back in the story. Then circle the right answer.

1. a. Saturday morning
   b. Wednesday morning

2. a. Tuesday morning
   b. Thursday morning

3. a. all day on Tuesday
   b. Monday morning

4. a. Friday at noon
   b. Saturday evening

5. a. early on Friday
   b. late Friday night

6. a. Friday afternoon
   b. early Sunday morning

Read this story to find out how long each child stayed at camp.

All the children came to summer camp on a big bus.

Sandy stayed at the camp on Saturday, Sunday, Monday, Tuesday, Wednesday, Thursday, Friday, Saturday, Sunday, Monday, Tuesday, Wednesday, Thursday, and Friday.

Beth was there on Saturday, Sunday, Monday, Tuesday, Wednesday, Thursday, and Friday. Then she went home.

Jay missed his mother and dad. He wanted to be back at home. Jay only stayed Saturday, Sunday, Monday, Tuesday, and Wednesday.

Les was at camp on Saturday, Sunday, Monday, Tuesday, Wednesday, Thursday, and Friday.

Write a letter under each picture to tell how long each child stayed at camp.

a. less than one week   b. one week
c. more than two weeks   d. two weeks

Les   Beth   Jay   Sandy

1. ____   2. ____   3. ____   4. ____

F **Draw lines to match these.**

1. place to sleep at camp   week

2. place to walk on   forgot

3. seven days   bunkhouse

4. hurt by a bee   campfire

5. not like others   camp

6. did not take   stung

7. a place to stay away from home   floor

                                         different

130

When Cathy and Jimmy went to camp, they wrote to their mom and dad. Read about their camp. Then read their letters. Which day were they telling about? Write the name of the day on the line.

On Sunday, they had a funny clown show. The next day they had a rock hunt. The kids put a frog in Sue's bed on Tuesday.

Jimmy had a cold on Wednesday. That day Cathy went on a long ride on a horse to Big Rock. The next day everyone cooked hot dogs around the campfire and sang songs.

Cathy lost her tennis shoes on Friday. Jimmy found some money the next day.

1. Hi!

   Today we found a frog by the lake. We put it in Sue's bed! You could hear her yell for a long way!

   Love,

   _____ Cathy

2. Dear Mom and Dad,

   My brother was sick today, but I rode to Big Rock on a horse. I am riding much better now.

   Love,

   _____ Cathy

3. Hello!

   The food here was bad today. After dinner we saw a clown show. It was so funny!

   Love,

   _____ Jimmy

4. Dear Family,

   I am taking care of my things, but Cathy is not. She lost her tennis shoes today.

   Love,

   _____ Jimmy

5. Dear Mom and Dad,

   We were going to ask you for some money, but now we don't need it. This morning Jim found five dollars in the woods. Please send the money next week.

   Thanks,

   Cathy and Jimmy

   _____

A mother raccoon had three hungry babies. These babies ate so much food that they cried for food all the time.

"Eat! Eat! Eat! All they want to do is eat!" said Mother Raccoon. "As soon as they get bigger, I will teach them how to find their own food."

She waited for the right time. On a Tuesday night in July, she took them to the pond. Mother Raccoon showed the babies how to catch fish. They got nine fish for a good dinner.

The very next night, Mother Raccoon took the babies to a field of corn. They did not make noise as they crept in. Each raccoon picked an ear of corn. Then they all went to the brook. They washed the corn in the water. Again they had a good meal.

On Thursday night, the raccoon family went to a garden. The garden was in back of a farmer's house. The raccoons crept under the fence to get in. What a good meal they had there! They ate lettuce, berries, cabbage, and carrots. They ate so much that they could not get back under the fence to go home. The fat raccoons crept by the farmer's front door. Then they went out an open gate.

"We're lucky that the farmer did not see us!" said Mother.

 <u>Underline</u> the right answer.

1. Which time of year did this story happen?

   a. summer   b. winter   c. fall

2. When did the raccoons go hunting for food?

    a. daytime   b. after dark   c. before dark

3. Why did the mother teach the babies to find their own food?

    a. She did not like the babies.

    b. She wanted them to help the farmer.

    c. She wanted them to take care of themselves.

4. Where did the raccoons go on Wednesday night?

    a. to a store

    b. to a pond

    c. to a field of corn

5. What do we know about the baby raccoons?

    a. They were hungry all the time.

    b. They were never hungry.

    c. They did not listen to their mother.

6. What did the raccoons do before they ate corn?

    a. They paid for it.

    b. They cleaned it in some water.

    c. They cooked it on a grill.

7. Why did the raccoons try not to make noise in the garden?

    a. They did not want to wake up the rabbits.

    b. They did not want to wake up the plants.

    c. They did not want to wake up the farmer.

8. How did the raccoons get out of the garden?

    a. They climbed over the fence.

    b. They walked past the farmer's door.

    c. They dug under the fence.

9. What is the best name for this story?

    a. The Baby Raccoons Learn Something New

    b. Mother Raccoon Learns Something New

    c. The Farmer's Big Garden

B Detective Sharp Eye wants you to put the story in the right order. Find the missing sentences in the box. Write the sentences on the lines where they belong.

---

a. They got fish at the pond.
b. They could not get under the fence again.
c. They crept into the field of corn.
d. They crept in to get some potatoes.

---

1. The raccoon babies were crying for food.
2. Mother Raccoon took them out hunting.

3. _____

4. _____

5. They crept into the farmer's garden.
6. They ate too much food.

7. _____

C Detective Sharp Eye wants you to tell when these things happened. <u>Underline</u> the right answer.

1. When did the raccoons wash and clean the corn?

   a. before they went into the field

   b. after they were in the field

2. When did the family go to the pond?

   a. before they went to the field of corn

   b. after they went to the garden

3. When did the babies cry for food?

   a. before they learned to find food

   b. after they learned to find food

4. When did they go into the farmer's garden?

   a. on Tuesday   b. on Wednesday   c. on Thursday

5. At noon, what do you think the raccoons were doing?

   a. washing food   b. sleeping   c. eating corn

D **Draw lines to match these.**

1. animals with rings on their tails   crept

2. moved slowly   field

3. ground where corn grows   raccoons

4. needing to eat   wash

5. red fruit   cabbage

6. an orange food   hungry

7. Mother's little ones   carrot

8. to clean food   babies

                                                             berries

E **What do you know about raccoons?**

1. Which one is a raccoon? Circle it.

   a.   b.   c.

2. How many paws does a raccoon have? _____

3. Do raccoons catch whales for food? _____

4. Can a raccoon fly? _____

5. Can a raccoon eat an ear of corn? _____

6. Do raccoons buy their fur coats in stores? _____

7. Do raccoons have rings on their fingers? _____

8. Do raccoons have rings on their tails? _____

9. Do raccoons have black fur by their eyes? _____

10. What will raccoons do to their food before they eat it?

    _____

11. Name six foods that raccoons will eat. _____

    _____

Read each story. Draw a line from the question to the answer.

Tiger Cat showed her kittens how to catch mice. The two kittens ran after a fat, gray mouse. But the mouse got away. The next time the kittens went after a mouse, they did catch it.

1. What happened first?

    a. A mouse got away from the kittens.

2. What happened next?

    b. Tiger Cat showed the kittens how to hunt.

3. What happened last?

    c. The kittens got a mouse.

Last week, Mr. Black helped Mr. and Mrs. Fell. Their car had stopped in the street. First, Mr. Fell tried to start the car. But it would not start. Then Mrs. Fell tried to start the car. It still did not start. Mr. Black got some gas in a can for Mr. and Mrs. Fell. They put the gas in. The car started.

4. What came first?

    a. The woman could not fix the car.

5. What came second?

    b. Mr. Black got some gas for Mr. and Mrs. Fell.

6. What came third?

    c. Mr. Fell could not fix the car.

7. What came last?

    d. The car stopped in the street.

For a long time, no one wanted to play baseball with Todd. He could not catch, hit, or run fast. Then Todd's dad showed him how to be a better player. Todd and his dad worked for five weeks. One day the children needed another player. They had to let Todd play. They got a surprise! Todd hit a home run!

8. What happened first?

    a. No one would let Todd play ball.

9. What happened second?

    b. Todd hit a home run.

10. What happened third?

    c. They let Todd play in the game.

11. What happened last?

    d. Todd and Dad worked on hitting.

Mr. Raccoon's Food

Mr. Raccoon liked to eat frogs better than anything. Frogs were easy to catch in the water. He could wash frogs and eat them quickly. But this week Mr. Raccoon was not lucky. He could not catch a frog. On Monday he ate only berries. The next night Mr. Raccoon had to fight with a little garden snake before he could eat it. On Wednesday he found some bugs on a tree to eat. He ate a thin, gray mouse on Thursday.

 Read Mr. Raccoon's story. Mr. Raccoon wrote a diary of what happened each day. Here are his diary pages and the things he wrote. Write what happened next to the right date. The first one is done for you.

a. The frogs are still too fast for me. I had nothing to eat but some black bugs!

b. The frogs were too quick for me. So I had some berries to eat.

c. All I could catch tonight was a thin mouse. The mouse was not very much to eat.

d. The snake tried to get away. What a fight! But I got it!

1. **Sunday, August 10 —** I want to eat some good frogs.

    Tomorrow I'll try to catch some frogs.

2. **Monday, August 11 —** _____

    _____

3. **Tuesday, August 12 —** _____

    _____

4. **Wednesday, August 13 —** _____

    _____

5. **Thursday, August 14 —** _____

    _____

The people of Butterfield have a car race on the second Saturday of October every year. Each family builds a small car and one child drives it. Winter Street is a big hill where they race.

Twelve cars were in the race last October. Mr. and Mrs. Press and their children had made a yellow car. It had a big black number eight on each side. Jenny Press was going to drive it.

Pop! The gun went off and the race started! Cars rolled down the big hill. People yelled for the car they liked best.

Car number six never got started. Its brake was stuck. Soon a front wheel fell off car number nine. It could not move. Car number three ran into car number four. Both cars were out of the race.

Jenny Press kept going. She was in front of all the other cars. Jenny looked behind her to see how far back the other cars were. That made her car slow down. Quickly, Chuck Rand in car number eleven went past Jenny.

Chuck won the race and Jenny came in right after him. Next came car number one with car number seven right beside it.

"It's a tie for third place!" yelled the people who watched.

Next came car two, then car twelve, then car five. Car number ten came in last.

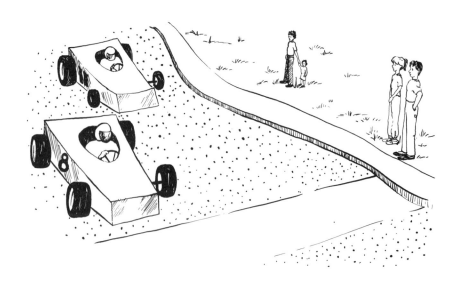

Underline the right answer.

1. What was the story about?

    a. horse racing in Butterfield

    b. bike racing on Winner Street

    c. car racing on Winter Street

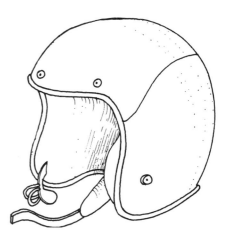

2. How often did they have this race?

    a. every year

    b. every month

    c. every week

3. What do you think Butterfield was?

    a. a big hill

    b. a school

    c. a small town

4. When was the race held?

    a. summer   b. fall   c. spring

5. How many cars finished the race?

    a. eight   b. twelve   c. four

6. Who came in first?

    a. Chuck Rand in number eleven

    b. Kevin in number one

    c. Jenny Press in number eight

7. Which car came in last?

    a. number two

    b. number ten

    c. number twelve

8. How did cars seven and one end the race?

    a. first and last

    b. at the same time

    c. They did not finish.

9. What kept Jenny from winning the race?

    a. The brake did not work.

    b. Her front wheel fell off.

    c. She looked back and slowed down.

10. What is the best name for this story?

    a. A Sled Race on Winter Hill

    b. Jenny Wins the Race

    c. Lost by a Look

B **This is a picture of the end of the race. The numbers on the cars are not clear. Put the right number on each car.**

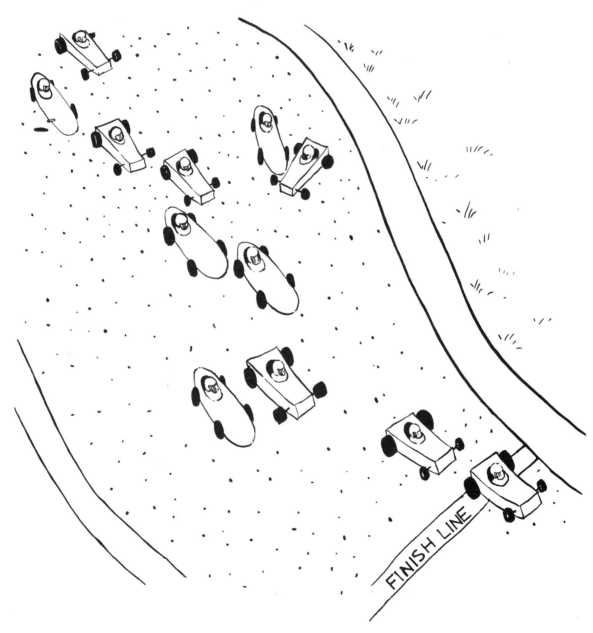

When did it happen? <u>Underline</u> the right answer.

1. When did car number twelve finish the race?

    a. before car number eight

    b. after car number eight

    c. in a tie with number eight

2. When did car number six come in?

    a. It did not finish the race.

    b. It came in last.

    c. It came in fifth.

3. When did car number five come in?

    a. It tied for third place.

    b. before car number eight

    c. after car number twelve

 Write a sentence to answer each question. Start the sentence with a capital letter and end it with a period. The first one has been started for you.

1. What happened to cars four and three?

    Cars four and three

    _____

2. Why didn't car number six get started?

    _____

3. Which cars were in a tie for third place?

    _____

4. Which car came in fourth place?

    _____

5. Which car came in sixth place?

    _____

6. Why didn't car nine finish the race?

    _____

E Draw lines to match these.

1. a day of the week

2. stopped so that it won't work

3. finish at the same time

4. tenth month of the year

5. It makes a car stop.

6. make the car go

7. in back of

8. next to

9. something on a car
   that rolls on the ground

10. three more than nine

twelve

October

stuck

Saturday

drive

tie

beside

wheel

behind

brake

second

F Which word belongs in the sentence? Write the word.

1. Families build cars for the race in _____.
   (Often, October, Other)

2. Before the race, Chuck washed his car to get it _____.
   (class, clean, close)

3. We must _____ by so we will not wake the baby.
   (creep, cry, camp)

4. The people _____ the gun start the race.
   (hair, happy, heard)

5. Jenny came in _____ in her yellow car.
   (started, Sunday, second)

6. The people saw the race from the _____.
   (field, filled, fish)

7. Each race car had four _____.
   (wheels, weeks, whales)

8. There was a _____ for third place in the car race.
   (tiny, tie, toy)

9. The cars stop at the end of the race by using

   their _____. (buttons, berries, brakes)

10. The car door was _____ and we could not open it. (stung, start, stuck)

 Ms. Black writes for the newspaper. Read what she wrote about last week in Butterfield.

On the first day, I went to a big fire on Winter Street. A house burned and a girl got three children out. On the second day, I went to a football game and the home team lost. I wrote a story about a bus crash on the third day. On the fourth day, I watched the Butterfield school children plant two trees in front of the school. A TV star came to Butterfield on the fifth day and I talked to him and took his picture. A truck full of fish turned over on Main Street on the sixth day.

Here are the dates when Ms. Black wrote stories. Put the right story name under the date when it happened.

1. **Monday, October 6**

   _____

2. **Tuesday, October 7**

   _____

3. **Wednesday, October 8**

   _____

4. **Thursday, October 9**

   _____

5. **Friday, October 10**

   _____

6. **Saturday, October 11**

   _____

Story Names
a. School Gets a New Look
b. House Burns on Winter Street
c. TV Star Comes to Town
d. 1,000 Fish Swim on Main Street
e. Butterfield Bees Lose 14 to 0
f. Bus Crashes

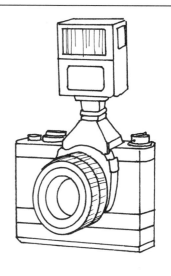

When Barby was born in October, Dad planted a dogwood tree. Every year Barby and the tree grew larger. When she was seven, Barby started to see that she and the dogwood tree kept changing together.

In May, Barby told Mom and Dad, "The dogwood tree has beautiful pink flowers on it now. I am different, too. I don't wear my winter coat anymore. I am wearing my light clothes."

Mom said, "Yes, the dogwood tree has flowers every spring. The days get warm and you change your clothes, too."

Barby kept watching the dogwood tree. By June, the tree had lost its pink flowers. It was wearing dark green leaves. Barby was not wearing a coat because the summer days were hot.

July, August, and part of September went by. One day Barby saw that the dogwood tree had red berries on it. The days were getting cooler and Barby was wearing her red jacket outdoors.

"Dogwood, we are eight years old today," Barby told the tree in October. The leaves and berries on the tree were redder. The fall days were colder and Barby wore her red coat outdoors.

All the leaves fell off the dogwood tree in November. Barby had to wear her hat, coat, scarf, and gloves to go outdoors. The days were cold through the winter months of December, January, and February.

"Isn't it strange?" said Barby to Mom and Dad. "The dogwood tree and I change with every season of the year. But in winter it wears nothing and I must wear many clothes to keep warm!"

A <u>Underline</u> the right answer.

1. What is this story about?

    a. Trees grow much faster than children.

    b. Barby has a birthday party every year.

    c. Every season people and trees change.

2. When did Dad plant the dogwood tree?

    a. when Barby was born

    b. when Barby was seven

    c. in the spring

3. Barby's birthday was in which month?

    a. September   b. October   c. May

4. The dogwood was planted at which time of year?

    a. spring   b. summer   c. fall

5. What is on a dogwood tree in the fall?

    a. flowers   b. berries   c. nothing

6. What is on a dogwood tree in the spring?

    a. flowers   b. berries   c. nothing

7. What were the days like in December, January, and February?

    a. very hot   b. very warm   c. very cold

8. What did Barby think was strange?

    a. The days were colder in the winter.

    b. The tree had nothing on it in the winter.

    c. Dad planted another dogwood tree.

9. What is the best name for this story?

    a. Barby and the Dogwood Change

    b. The Dogwood Leaves

    c. Barby's New Red Coat

B Draw lines to match these.

1. came into life

2. not inside the house

3. bigger

4. becoming different

5. a short coat

6. something to keep hands warm

7. something to keep the neck warm

8. one of four times of the year

changing

born

larger

outdoors

scarf

November

season

jacket

gloves

C What time of year is it? Write the name of the season over each picture.

The Four Seasons			
winter	spring	summer	fall

1. _____

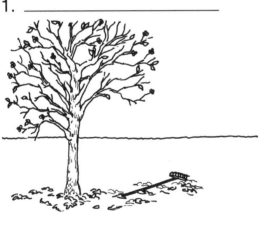

2. _____

3. _____

4. _____

146

Write the name of the season that each story tells about.

The Four Seasons			
winter	spring	summer	fall

1. This season is very, very hot. People want to stay under the trees to keep cool. Windows in houses are left open. Everyone wants cold drinks and ice cream.

   _____

2. It is so cold outside, people must keep their houses warm inside. Some people burn wood. Schools must be kept warm, too. People wear coats, hats, and gloves outdoors. Dogs get thick fur to keep them warm.

   _____

3. Green leaves change into beautiful red, yellow, orange, and brown leaves. Then they fall to the ground. Nuts fall from trees, too. Squirrels save the nuts.

   _____

4. Tiny new green leaves start to come out on trees and plants. Beautiful flowers come out on some trees. Many bugs and animals are born.

   _____

5. The days are getting cooler. The days are not as long as they were. Leaves cover the ground. People rake the leaves. Children start back to school for another year.

   _____

6. Birds fly back from their winter homes. They build new nests and lay eggs. The rain turns the grass green. New flowers start to push up out of the ground. Days are getting warmer.

   _____

E Write the name of the month that comes next. Use the list of months.

Twelve Months of a Year			
January	February	March	April
May	June	July	August
September	October	November	December

1. September, _____, November

2. May, _____, _____, August

3. February, _____, April, _____

4. July, _____, September, _____

5. March, _____, _____, June

6. December, _____, _____

F When did these things happen? Look back at the story for help.

January	February	March	April
May	June	July	August
September	October	November	December

1. Put a black **X** on the three winter months when Barby must wear warm clothes.
2. Put a yellow star on the month when Barby was born.
3. Put a brown circle around the month when the dogwood tree had pink flowers.
4. Put red berries on the fall month when Barby saw that the dogwood tree had berries.
5. Put a blue box on the last month of the year.
6. Put a purple ✔ on the summer month when the dogwood tree lost its pink flowers.
7. Put a red circle around the month of your birthday.

Mother started a baby book when Barby was born. Mother wanted to remember the dates when Barby started to learn new things. Here is part of the baby book. Read this story. Then write the right things next to each date.

Five months after Barby was born, she learned to sit up. The next month she learned how to drink from a cup.

Barby learned how to crawl when she was seven months old. At eight months, Barby could stand by herself.

Four months later, Barby was one year old. She learned to walk alone for the first time.

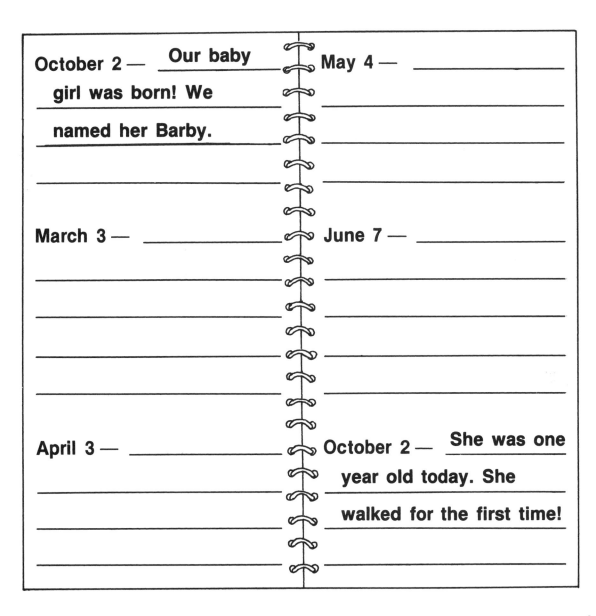

October 2 — Our baby girl was born! We named her Barby.

March 3 — _____

April 3 — _____

May 4 — _____

June 7 — _____

October 2 — She was one year old today. She walked for the first time!

SKILLS REVIEW (Stories 22–26)

 A These children are in the same class. They were all born the same year. The name of the month when the child was born is under each picture.

Danny	Sam	Ruth	Wen	Ella	Chang
February	June	March	January	May	April

Now, write the children's names in order, starting with the oldest. Write the month the child was born next to the name.

	Name	**Month Born**
1.	Wen	— January
2.	_____	— _____
3.	_____	— _____
4.	_____	— _____
5.	_____	— _____
6.	_____	— _____

7. Which two were born after Chang? _____ and _____

8. Which child was born before Danny? _____

9. Which child is the oldest? _____

10. Which child was born last? _____

B Which word fits the sentence? Write the word.

1. Cats must _____ milk with their tongues to drink.
   sink   lick   pick

2. We stood on the sidewalk to _____ the cars go by.
   whisker   which   watch

3. My tongue is in my _____.
    month   mouse   mouth

4. Never talk to _____ people on the street.
    change   orange   strange

5. Many red _____ fell off the tree this fall.
    berries   babies   brooms

6. We had to _____ to make you hear us.
    yellow   yell   yesterday

7. The children will have a _____ after school.
    middle   midnight   meeting

8. There are four _____ in one year.
    seasons   seconds   sidewalks

9. A dogwood tree is _____ our house.
    beside   between   because

C **Which one comes next? Pick a word from the box to write.**

spring	fall	Tuesday	Thursday
January	July	grandfather	first
noon	night	fifth	

1. Monday, _____, Wednesday

2. _____, second, third, fourth

3. morning, _____, afternoon, evening

4. May, June, _____, August

5. winter, _____, summer, fall

6. eighth, seventh, sixth, _____

7. December, _____, February

8. _____, Friday, Saturday

Read this story. Under it is Scott's book where he puts good pictures. Can you help fix the book? First, put the dates in the book. Then, find the pictures on the next page. Put the letter and name of each picture under the right date in the book. The first one is done for you.

On Thursday night, the second of September, Scott took a picture of a family of raccoons as they crept into a field to get a meal of sweet corn.

On September third, Scott saw a snake resting beside the tomato plants near the fence.

"That will make a good picture," said Scott. Snap!

The next morning Scott walked to Tenth Street. He saw a big truck stuck in the mud on a hill. Snap!

On Sunday, the fifth of September, Scott saw a little red flower coming up in a crack in the sidewalk. Snap!

The next afternoon Scott took a picture of two teams playing a football game. Snap!

On Tuesday he took a picture of a house that was built many years ago.

Scott's Picture Book

1. Thursday, September **2**	4. Sunday, September ____
b. A Good Meal	
2. Friday, September ____	5. Monday, September ____
3. Saturday, September ____	6. Tuesday, September ____

Scott's Pictures

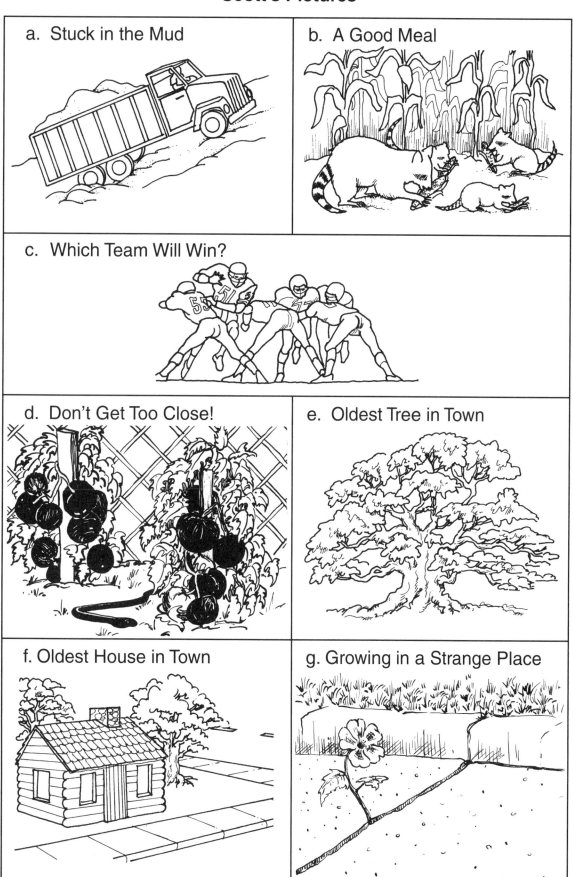

a. Stuck in the Mud

b. A Good Meal

c. Which Team Will Win?

d. Don't Get Too Close!

e. Oldest Tree in Town

f. Oldest House in Town

g. Growing in a Strange Place

Answer Key

Story 1
pages 7–10

A 1. b   5. a
    2. c   6. a
    3. b   7. c
    4. a   8. b

B 1. heard   5. voice
    2. suit   6. feathers
    3. ice   7. several
    4. skinny   8. stomach

C Correct order: 2, 3, 1

D 2. voice   5. warm
    3. suit   6. bills
    4. each

Story 2
pages 11–14

A 1. a   4. b
    2. c   5. c
    3. c

B 1. followed   3. waved
    2. flippers   4. parents

C 1. X   4. X
    2. X   5. ✔
    3. ✔   6. ✔

D Make sure lines are drawn to the correct parts of the penguin.

E 1. flippers   3. flash
    2. same   4. gills

Story 3
pages 15–18

A 1. b   5. b
    2. c   6. b
    3. c   7. c
    4. a   8. a

B 1. hide   4. eleven
    2. other   5. back
    3. asked

C Correct order: 4, 5, 2, 3, 1

D 1. no   5. yes
    2. yes   6. no
    3. no   7. yes
    4. yes

Story 4
pages 19–22

A 1. c   5. a
    2. b   6. b
    3. b   7. c
    4. c   8. c

B 1. beautiful   5. float
    2. melts   6. outdoors
    3. carrot   7. sink
    4. nose

C 2. That's   4. me
    3. Let`s   5. We

D Y, S, C, no mark, K

Story 5
pages 23–26

A 1. b   4. c
    2. c   5. b
    3. a   6. b

B Color the boats and write the names of the colors.
    1. pink   3. purple
    2. green   4. orange

C 1. lake   5. third
    2. bumped   6. winner
    3. fire   7. across
    4. orange   8. line

D 2. butter   5. tree
    3. boat   6. second
    4. third   7. fire

E Make sure the directions for coloring and marking were followed.

Skills Review (Stories 1–5)
pages 27–30

A 1. b
    2. c
    3. c

B Make sure lines were drawn to the correct pictures.

C 1. Pedro   4. Sam
    2. Sally   5. Jill
    3. Ann   6. Dan

D 1. water   3. a dog
    2. mouth   4. a cold

E 1. third   6. melts
    2. across   7. wins
    3. stomach   8. feathers
    4. gills   9. fur
    5. sink   10. last

Story 6
pages 31–34

A 1. c   4. c
    2. c   5. b
    3. a   6. c

B 1. understand   5. home run
    2. popcorn   6. brother
    3. lap   7. outdoors
    4. batter

C 1. Jay   4. Janet
    2. Janet   5. Jay
    3. Jay

D 1. c   2. j   3. g
    4. b   5. e   6. a
    7. d   8. i   9. h

Story 7
pages 35–38

A 1. b   5. a
    2. c   6. b
    3. b   7. c
    4. c   8. c

B 1. laughed   5. seed
    2. pumpkin   6. became
    3. woman   7. ground
    4. pretty   8. planting

C 1. a   4. b
    2. b   5. a
    3. b   6. a

Story 8
pages 39–42

A 1. c   4. b
    2. a   5. c
    3. b   6. b

B 1. Thursday   5. woods
    2. tracks   6. skunk
    3. fallen   7. funny
    4. followed

154

C
1. first picture 5. no
2. four 6. no
3. no 7. yes
4. no 8. no

D
1. hid 4. boots
2. smell 5. tracks
3. fallen

Story 9
pages 43–46

A
1. c 4. a
2. a 5. b
3. b 6. c

B
1. good 6. day
2. cry 7. new
3. before 8. hot
4. sad 9. yes
5. over

C
1. cat 3. friend
2. woods 4. nose

D
1. swim 4. smell
2. eating 5. hunt
3. stay 6. think

Story 10
pages 47–50

A
1. b 6. c
2. a 7. c
3. c 8. c
4. c 9. c
5. b

B
1. worm 4. hold
2. grandmother 5. close
3. Friday 6. left

C
1. c 4. a
2. c 5. a
3. b

Skills Review
(Stories 6–10)
pages 51–54

A
1. people 2. foods
3. places 4. colors

B
1. brother 4. woman
2. laughed 5. Thursday
3. outdoors 6. close

C
1. first picture 6. no
2. no 7. no
3. no 8. yes
4. yes 9. no
5. yes

D
1. sun 2. milk
3. turtle 4. squirrel

E
1. and 2.: hold
3. and 4.: plant
5. and 6.: fall

F
1. Jack 4. Tom
2. Betty 5. Jill
3. Bob

G
1. a 4. b
2. b 5. a
3. a

Story 11
pages 55–58

A
1. b 5. b
2. c 6. b
3. a 7. c
4. b

B
1. Karen
2. Ann
3. Mai

C
1. mall 5. tiny
2. pizza 6. eleven
3. large 7. morning
4. picture 8. door

D
1. a 4. b
2. b 5. a
3. b

Story 12
pages 59–62

A
1. b 4. a
2. c 5. a
3. b 6. c

B
1. tub 4. hall
2. hid 5. aunt
3. heard 6. yard

C
1. 7 4. 4
2. 10 5. The New Birdbath
3. 4

D
1. living room
2. yard
3. second
4. bath
5. Peggy's bedroom

Story 13
pages 63–66

A
1. a 5. a
2. a 6. a
3. c 7. c
4. b 8. c

B
1. fool 5. bite
2. pad 6. tongue
3. quick 7. tickle
4. stuck

C
1. hands 3. a
2. eyes

Story 14
pages 67–70

A
1. b 4. b
2. a 5. c
3. a 6. b

B
1. sister 5. friends
2. birthday 6. candle
3. enough 7. us
4. buy 8. counted

C
1. d 5. b
2. a 6. h
3. f 7. e
4. c

D
1. her next birthday
2. bottom
3. enough
4. hole
5. candles

Story 15
pages 71–74

A
1. c 5. a
2. b 6. b
3. c 7. a
4. c

B
1. snake 4. bite
2. other 5. smell
3. afraid

155

C Correct order: 1, 3, 4, 2

D Story 1: d   Story 3: e
Story 2: a   Story 4: b

Story 16
pages 75–78

A 1. a   5. c
2. c   6. b
3. c   7. a
4. a   8. b

B 1. candy   Friday
2. cake   Monday
3. bread   Wednesday
4. orange   Tuesday
5. apple   Thursday

C 1. d   2. a
3. i   4. j
5. c   6. h
7. f   8. e

Skills Review
(Stories 11–16)
pages 79–83

A 1. c, d
2. b, c
3. a, c, d

B 1. a   4. b
2. b   5. a
3. a

C 1. doughnut
2. banana
3. fig
4. before banana

D 1. a   4. b
2. b   5. c
3. c

E 1. d   4. a
2. b   5. e
3. f   6. g

F 1. squirrel   4. snake
2. tiger   5. fish
3. ant

Story 17
pages 84–89

A 1. popular   5. mounted
2. stall   6. mane
3. hind   7. gallop
4. gentle   8. wild

B 1. c   5. c
2. b   6. a
3. b   7. b
4. a

C 1. b   6. e
2. a   7. h
3. c   8. g
4. d   9. j
5. f   10. i

D 1. ears   2. mane
3. nose   4. saddle
5. mouth   6. tail
7. reins   8. legs

E 1. What Mounted Police Wore
2. How the Mounted Police Are
Trained

F 1. a   4. b
2. c   5. a
3. c

Story 18
pages 90–95

A 1. b   5. b
2. a   6. b
3. b   7. c
4. c

B 1. a. Thursday
b. April
c. warm
d. Discuss responses.
2. a. Friday
b. two birds
c. on the window sill
3. a. three
b. three weeks
4. when the sun was coming up
a. morning
b. so no one would hear her
5. third floor

C 1. X   6. X
2. X   7. X
3. ✔   8. ✔
4. ✔   9. ✔
5. X   10. X

D 1. lock   2. always
3. secret   4. shut
5. hungry   6. wonderful
7. quiet   8. frighten

Story 19
pages 96–101

A 1. c   5. a
2. c   6. b
3. b   7. c
4. c   8. b

B 1. c   4. e
2. d   5. b
3. a

C 1. Mr. Sharp Eye
2. Ms. Boone
3. Pam Panda

D 1. b   4. c
2. c   5. a
3. c   6. a

E 1. a
2. c
3. c

F 1. b
2. a
3. a

Story 20
pages 102–107

A 1. b   5. a
2. b   6. a
3. c   7. a
4. a   8. b

B 1. a. 2
b. 3
c. 4
d. Cross out two faces.
e. 9
2. a. 5:00
b. 7:00
c. 2
3. a. Ed, Tommy, Jeff
b. Box the first picture.
4. hot dogs, hamburgers,
potatoes, corn, ice cream
5. The children ate until they were
full.
6. grill
7. flowers (Check drawings.)

C 1. cookout   5. treasure
2. potato   6. shape
3. hamburger   7. class
4. grill

156

D 1. b 　　 5. a
　　 2. c 　　 6. c
　　 3. b 　　 7. b
　　 4. a

E 1. by the house
　　 2. between two rocks
　　 3. to the doghouse
　　 4. to the fence
　　 5. by the flowers
　　 6. to the swing set
　　 7. to the fence
　　 8. by the rocks
　　 9. Answers will vary.
　　 10. Mark X on the treasure chest
　　　　 between the rocks.

Story 21
pages 108–113

A 1. a 　　 5. a
　　 2. b 　　 6. a
　　 3. b 　　 7. b
　　 4. a 　　 8. c

B 1. Lee 　　 4. dollars
　　 2. came 　　 5. played
　　 3. shell

C 1. 1 　　 4. 3
　　 2. 4 　　 5. 5
　　 3. 3 　　 6. 2

D 1. Lee 　　 4. Lee
　　 2. a friend 　　 5. the sea
　　 3. Lee

E 1. b 　　 4. d
　　 2. f 　　 5. e
　　 3. a

F Cross out the fourth and last sentences and rewrite the paragraph.

G 1. g 　　 2. e
　　 3. f 　　 4. a
　　 5. c 　　 6. b

H 1. b 　　 4. a
　　 2. d 　　 5. c
　　 3. e

I 1. 9 　　 6. 0
　　 2. water 　　 7. no
　　 3. 2 　　 8. yes
　　 4. 0 　　 9. on the bottom
　　 5. 9

Skills Review
(Stories 17–21)
pages 114–119

A 1. 3
　　 2. food
　　 3. store
　　 4. bikes
　　 5. They
　　 6. Milly, Ron
　　 7. b
　　 8. a
　　 9. bread, hamburger meat, milk,
　　　　 ice cream
　　 10. 1
　　 11. 1
　　 12. 3
　　 13. 1
　　 14. 3
　　 15. 2
　　 16. a. They carried the food in
　　　　　 baskets on their bikes.
　　　　 b. the picture

B Cross out sentence 2. Then rewrite sentences in this order: 3, 4, 5, 1.

C 1. circle b
　　 2. circle c
　　 3. check ✔ b
　　 4. circle c
　　 5. check ✔ a

D Make sure the directions for coloring and marking the pictures were followed.

E 1. a 　　 4. c
　　 2. b 　　 5. e
　　 3. d 　　 6. f

F 1. b 　　 3. a
　　 2. c 　　 4. b

G 1. check 　　 4. back
　　 2. light 　　 5. check
　　 3. light

H 1. a 　　 2. c

I 1. main 　　 6. rains
　　 2. rains 　　 7. checks
　　 3. reins 　　 8. mane
　　 4. mane 　　 9. reins
　　 5. checks

Story 22
pages 120–125

A 1. c 　　 5. a
　　 2. c 　　 6. c
　　 3. b 　　 7. b
　　 4. c

B 1. Wow 　　 4. fun
　　 2. play 　　 5. hit
　　 3. whale 　　 6. 4

C 1. 4 　　 7. 3
　　 2. 1 　　 8. 7
　　 3. 3 　　 9. 2
　　 4. 6 　　 10. 5
　　 5. 4 　　 11. 4
　　 6. 5 　　 12. 6

D 1. spray 　　 5. small
　　 2. through 　　 6. lucky
　　 3. learn 　　 7. hiding
　　 4. together 　　 8. noise

E 1. and 2.: fish
　　 3. and 4.: air

F Write the paragraph omitting sentence 2.

G 1. ! 　　 5. !
　　 2. ? 　　 6. .
　　 3. . 　　 7. !
　　 4. ? 　　 8. ?

H 1. b 　　 3. b
　　 2. a 　　 4. a

Story 23
pages 126–131

A 1. c 　　 5. b
　　 2. b 　　 6. a
　　 3. b 　　 7. c
　　 4. a 　　 8. a

B 1. Friday
　　 2. Monday, Wednesday
　　 3. Thursday, Friday
　　 4. Friday, Sunday
　　 5. Tuesday, Wednesday
　　 6. evening
　　 7. morning, night
　　 8. night, noon

C Make sure the directions for coloring and marking were followed.

D 1. b 　　 2. b
　　 3. a 　　 4. b
　　 5. a 　　 6. a

E 1. b 3. a
2. b 4. d

F 1. bunkhouse 5. different
2. floor 6. forgot
3. week 7. camp
4. stung

G 1. Tuesday 2. Wednesday
3. Sunday 4. Friday
5. Saturday

Story 24
pages 132–137

A 1. a 4. c 7. c
2. b 5. a 8. b
3. c 6. b 9. a

B 3. They got fish at the pond.
4. They crept into the field of corn.
7. They could not get under the fence again.

C 1. b 3. a 5. b
2. a 4. c

D 1. raccoons 5. berries
2. crept 6. carrot
3. field 7. babies
4. hungry 8. wash

E 1. b
2. 4 6. no
3. no 7. no
4. no 8. yes
5. yes 9. yes
10. They will dip their food in water.
11. fish, corn, lettuce, berries, cabbage, carrots

F 1. b 5. c 9. d
2. a 6. a 10. c
3. c 7. b 11. b
4. d 8. a

G 2. b 4. a
3. d 5. c

Story 25
pages 138–143

A 1. c 5. a 9. c
2. a 6. a 10. c
3. c 7. b
4. b 8. b

B Number cars from top to bottom.
6, 9, 10, 5, 3, 4, 12, 2, 1 or 7, 7 or 1, 8, 11

C 1. b 3. c
2. a

D 1. Cars four and three ran into each other.
2. The brake was stuck on number six.
3. Cars one and seven were in a tie for third place.
4. Car two came in fourth.
5. Car five came in sixth place.
6. A front wheel fell off car nine.

E 1. Saturday 6. drive
2. stuck 7. behind
3. tie 8. beside
4. October 9. wheel
5. brake 10. twelve

F 1. October 6. field
2. clean 7. wheels
3. creep 8. tie
4. heard 9. brakes
5. second 10. stuck

G 1. House Burns on Winter Street
2. Butterfield Bees Lose 14 to 0
3. Bus Crashes
4. School Gets a New Look
5. TV Star Comes to Town
6. 1,000 Fish Swim on Main Street

Story 26
pages 144–149

A 1. c 4. c 7. c
2. a 5. b 8. b
3. b 6. a 9. a

B 1. born 5. jacket
2. outdoors 6. gloves
3. larger 7. scarf
4. changing 8. season

C 1. fall 2. spring
3. summer 4. winter

D 1. summer 4. spring
2. winter 5. fall
3. fall 6. spring

E 1. October
2. June, July
3. March, May
4. August, October
5. April, May
6. January, February

F Make sure the directions for coloring and marking were followed.

G **October 2**—Our baby girl was born! We named her Barby.
March 3—Barby learned how to sit up.
April 3—Barby learned how to drink from a cup.
May 4—Barby learned how to crawl.
June 7—Barby learned how to stand by herself.
October 2—She was one year old today. She walked for the first time!

Skills Review
(Stories 22–26)
pages 150–153

A 2. Danny—February
3. Ruth—March 7. Ella, Sam
4. Chang—April 8. Wen
5. Ella—May 9. Wen
6. Sam—June 10. Sam

B 1. lick 6. yell
2. watch 7. meeting
3. mouth 8. seasons
4. strange 9. beside
5. berries

C 1. Tuesday 5. spring
2. first 6. fifth
3. noon 7. January
4. July 8. Thursday

D 2. 3, d. Don't Get Too Close!
3. 4, a. Stuck in the Mud
4. 5, g. Growing in a Strange Place
5. 6, c. Which Team Will Win?
6. 7, f. Oldest House in Town